Risk Management
The Open Group Guide

Other publications by Van Haren Publishing

Van Haren Publishing (VHP) specializes in titles on Best Practices, methods and standards within four domains:
- IT management
- Architecture (Enterprise and IT)
- Business management and
- Project management

Van Haren Publishing offers a wide collection of whitepapers, templates, free e-books, trainer material etc. in the **VHP Freezone**: freezone.vanharen.net

VHP is also publisher on behalf of leading organizations and companies:
ASLBiSL Foundation, CA, Centre Henri Tudor, Gaming Works, Getronics, IACCM, IAOP, IPMA-NL, ITSqc, NAF, Ngi, PMI-NL, PON, Quint, The Open Group, The Sox Institute

Topics are (per domain):

IT (Service) Management / IT Governance	Architecture (Enterprise and IT)	Project/Programme/ Risk Management
ABC of ICT	Archimate®	A4-Projectmanagement
ASL	GEA®	ICB / NCB
BiSL	SOA	MINCE®
CATS	TOGAF®	M_o_R®
CMMI		MSP™
CoBIT	**Business Management**	P3O
ISO 17799	CMMI	*PMBOK® Guide*
ISO 27001	Contract Management	PRINCE2®
ISO 27002	EFQM	
ISO/IEC 20000	eSCM	
ISPL	ISA-95	
IT Service CMM	ISO 9000	
ITIL® V3	ISO 9001:2000	
ITSM	OPBOK	
MOF	Outsourcing	
MSF	SAP	
SABSA	SixSigma	
	SOX	
	SqEME®	

For the latest information on VHP publications, visit our website: www.vanharen.net, or freezone.vanharen.net for free whitepapers, templates and e-books.

Risk Management
The Open Group Guide

THE Open GROUP

Van Haren
PUBLISHING

Colofon

Title:	Risk Management - The Open Group Guide
A Publication of:	The Open Group
Authors:	The Open Group
Editors:	Ian Dobson and Jim Hietala
Publisher:	Van Haren Publishing, Zaltbommel, www.vanharen.net
ISBN:	978 90 8753 663 3
Edition:	First edition, first impression, April 2011
Design and Layout:	CO2 Premedia bv, Amersfoort – NL
Copyright:	© The Open Group, 2011

For any further enquiries about Van Haren Publishing, please send an e-mail to: info@vanharen.net

© All rights reserved.

No part of this publication may be reproduced, stored in a retrieval system, or transmitted, in any form or by any means, electronic, mechanical, photocopying, recording, or otherwise, without the prior permission of the copyright owner.

The views expressed in this document are not necessarily those of any particular member of The Open Group.

Comments relating to the material contained in this document may be submitted to:
The Open Group
Apex Plaza, Forbury Road
Reading
Berkshire RG1 1AX
United Kingdom
or by electronic mail to:

ogspecs@opengroup.org

Preface

This book has been developed by **The Open Group,** a vendor-neutral and technology-neutral consortium, whose vision of Boundaryless Information Flow™ will enable access to integrated information within and between enterprises based on open standards and global interoperability. The Open Group works with customers, suppliers, consortia, and other standards bodies. Its role is to capture, understand, and address current and emerging requirements, establish policies, and share best practices; to facilitate interoperability, develop consensus, and evolve and integrate specifications and Open Source technologies; to offer a comprehensive set of services to enhance the operational efficiency of consortia; and to operate the industry's premier certification service, including UNIX® certification.

Further information on The Open Group is available at www.opengroup.org.

The Open Group has over 15 years' experience in developing and operating certification programs and has extensive experience developing and facilitating industry adoption of test suites used to validate conformance to an open standard or specification.

More information is available at www.opengroup.org/certification.

The Open Group publishes a wide range of technical documentation, the main part of which is focused on development of Technical and Product Standards and Guides, but which also includes white papers, technical studies, branding and testing documentation, and business titles. Full details and a catalog are available at www.opengroup.org/bookstore.

Trademarks

Boundaryless Information Flow™ is a trademark and ArchiMate®, Jericho Forum®, Making Standards Work®, Motif®, OSF/1®, The Open Group®, TOGAF®, UNIX®, and the "X" device are registered trademarks of The Open Group in the United States and other countries.

COBIT® is a registered trademark of the Information Systems Audit and Control Association and the IT Governance Institute.

ITIL® is a registered trademark of the Office of Government Commerce in the United Kingdom and other countries.

OCTAVE® (Operationally Critical Threat, Asset, and Vulnerability Evaluation) is a registered trademark of CERT at Carnegie Mellon University (see www.cert.org/octave).

The Open Group acknowledges that there may be other brand, company, and product names used in this document that may be covered by trademark protection and advises the reader to verify them independently.

Acknowledgements

Part 1: The Open Group Technical Standard: Risk Taxonomy
The Open Group gratefully acknowledges the contribution of:
- Alex Hutton, CEO, Risk Management Insight
- Jack Jones, CTO, Risk Management Insight

for contributing their FAIR (Factor Analysis of Information Risk) development work into the Security Forum of The Open Group, and their continued support in guiding the Security Forum members through The Open Group development and approval process to publish this Risk Taxonomy standard. The Open Group also acknowledges the members of its Security Forum who contributed to its development.

Part 2: The Open Group - Technical Guide
Requirements for Risk Assessment Methodologies
The Open Group gratefully acknowledges the contribution of:
- Alex Hutton, CEO, Risk Management Insight
  (www.riskmanagementinsight.com)

- Jack Jones, CTO, Risk Management Insight and the members of The Open Group Security Forum who contributed to its development.

Part 3: The Open Group Technical Guide FAIR–ISO/IEC 27005 Cookbook

The Open Group gratefully acknowledges the contribution of lead authors:
- Christopher Carlson, The Boeing Company
- Alex Hutton, Risk Management Insight, with the valued support of contributing author
- Anastasia Gilliam, Independent Consultant and the members of The Open Group Security Forum who contributed to its development.

References

The following documents are referenced in Part 1: The Open Group Technical Standard: **Risk Taxonomy**:
- An Introduction to Factor Analysis of Information Risk (FAIR), Risk Management Insight LLC, November 2006; refer to www.riskmanagementinsight.com.
- Methods for the Identification of Emerging and Future Risks, European Network and Information Security Agency (ENISA), November 2007; refer to www.enisa.europa.eu/doc/pdf/deliverables/EFR_Methods_Identification_200804.pdf.
- Operationally Critical Threat, Asset, and Vulnerability Evaluation (OCTAVE), US-CERT; refer to www.cert.org/octave.
- A Taxonomy of Computer Program Security Flaws, with Examples, Naval Research Laboratory, September 1994; refer to http://chacs.nrl.navy.mil/publications.

The following documents are referenced in Part 2: The Open Group Technical Guide: **Requirements for Risk Assessment Methodologies**:
- COBIT (Control Objectives for Information and related Technology), Information Systems Audit and Control Association (ISACA); refer to www.isaca.org
- COSO (Committee of Sponsoring Organizations) Enterprise Risk Management Framework; refer to www.coso.org
- ISO/IEC 27002:2005: Information Technology – Security Techniques – Code of Practice for Information Security Management

- ITIL (Information Technology Infrastructure Library); refer to www.itil-officialsite.com/home
- OCTAVE (Operationally Critical Threat, Asset, and Vulnerability Evaluation); refer to www.cert.org/octave
- Risk Taxonomy Technical Standard, January 2009 (ISBN: 1-931624-77-1, C081), published by The Open Group
- FAIR - ISO/IEC 27005 Cookbook Technical Guide, November 2010 (ISBN: 1-931624-87-9, C103), published by The Open Group

The following documents are referenced in Part 3: The Open Group **Technical Guide FAIR–ISO/IEC 27005 Cookbook:**
- ISO/IEC 27005:2008: Information Technology – Security Techniques – Information Security Risk Management.
- ISO/IEC 27001:2005: Information Technoloy – Security Techniques – Information Security Management System – Requirements (ISMS)
- ISO/IEC 27002:2005: Information Technology – Security Techniques – Code of Practice for Information Security Management (Controls)
- Technical Standard: Risk Taxonomy (C081, ISBN: 1-931624-77-1), January 2009, published by The Open Group
- Technical Guide: Requirements for Risk Assessment Methodologies (G081, ISBN: 1-931624-78-X), January 2009, published by The Open Group

Contents

Preface V
Acknowledgements VI
References VII
Introduction XIII

Part 1 The Open Group Technical Standard
Risk Taxonomy   1

Chapter 1 Introduction to risk taxonomy   2
1.1 Scope 2
1.2 Purpose/objective 3
1.3 Context 3
1.4 The risk language gap 3
1.5 Using FAIR with other risk assessment frameworks 5
    1.5.1 The ability of a FAIR-based approach to complement other standards 5
    1.5.2 An example: using FAIR with OCTAVE 5
    1.5.3 Conclusion 6

Chapter 2 Business case for a risk taxonomy   7
2.1 What makes this the standard of choice? 9
2.2 Who should use this Technical Standard? 10
2.3 Related dependencies 11

Chapter 3 Risk management model   12
3.1 Risk assessment approach 12
3.2 Why is a tightly-defined taxonomy critical? 12

Chapter 4 Functional aspects   13
4.1 What is defined? 13
4.2 What is in/out of scope and why? 13
4.3 How should it be used? 13

Chapter 5 Technical aspects — 14
- 5.1 Risk taxonomy overview 14
- 5.2 Component definitions 15
  - 5.2.1 Risk 15
  - 5.2.2 Loss Event Frequency (LEF) 15
  - 5.2.3 Threat Event Frequency (TEF) 16
  - 5.2.4 Contact 16
  - 5.2.5 Action 17
  - 5.2.6 Vulnerability 17
  - 5.2.7 Threat Capability 19
  - 5.2.8 Control Strength (CS) 19
  - 5.2.9 Probable Loss Magnitude (PLM) 20
  - 5.2.10 Forms of loss 21
  - 5.2.11 Loss factors 22
  - 5.2.12 Primary loss factors 23
  - 5.2.13 Secondary loss factors 26

Chapter 6 Example application — 31
- 6.1 The scenario 31
- 6.2 The analysis: FAIR basic risk assessment methodology 31
  - 6.2.1 Stage 1: Identify scenario components 32
  - 6.2.2 Stage 2: Evaluate Loss Event Frequency (LEF) 33
  - 6.2.3 Stage 3: Evaluate Probable Loss Magnitude (PLM) 36
  - 6.2.4 Stage 4: Derive and articulate risk 41
- 6.3 Further information 42

Appendix A Risk taxonomy considerations — 43
- A.1 Complexity of the model 43
- A.2 Availability of data 44
- A.3 Iterative risk analyses 44
- A.4 Perspective 45

Part 2 The Open Group Technical Guide
Requirements for risk assessment methodologies — 47

Chapter 1 Introduction to requirements for risk assessment methodologies — 48
1.1 Business case for risk assessment methodologies 48
1.2 Scope 49
1.3 Using this Technical Guide 49
1.4 Definition of terms 49
1.5 Key operating assumptions 50

Chapter 2 What makes a good risk assessment methodology? — 51
2.1 Key component: taxonomy 51
2.2 Key risk assessment traits 51
    2.2.1 Probabilistic 51
    2.2.2 Accurate 52
    2.2.3 Consistent (repeatable) 53
    2.2.4 Defensible 53
    2.2.5 Logical 53
    2.2.6 Risk-focused 54
    2.2.7 Concise and meaningful 54
    2.2.8 Feasible 54
    2.2.9 Actionable 55
    2.2.10 Prioritized 55
    2.2.11 Important note 55

Chapter 3 Risk assessment methodology considerations — 56
3.1 Use of qualitative versus quantitative scales 56
    3.1.1 When is using numbers not quantitative? 57
3.2 Measurement scales 57
    3.2.1 Nominal scale 57
    3.2.2 Ordinal scale 57
    3.2.3 Interval scale 57
    3.2.4 Ratio scale 58
    3.2.5 Important note 58

3.3	How frequent is 'likely'?		58
3.4	Risk and the data owners		59

Chapter 4 Assessment elements   60
4.1	Identifying risk issues		60
	4.1.1	Interviews and questionnaires	60
	4.1.2	Testing	61
	4.1.3	Sampling	62
	4.1.4	Types of sampling	62
4.2	Evaluating the severity/significance of risk issues		62
4.3	Identifying the root cause of risk issues		63
4.4	Identifying cost-effective solution options		63
4.5	Communicating the results to management		64
	4.5.1	What to communicate	64
	4.5.2	How to communicate	64

Part 3 The Open Group Technical Guide
FAIR–ISO/IEC 27005 Cookbook   67

Chapter 1 Introduction to the FAIR–ISO/IEC 27005 Cookbook   68
1.1	Purpose	68
1.2	Scope	68
1.3	Intended audience	68
1.4	Operating assumptions	69
1.5	Using this Cookbook	69

Chapter 2 How to manage risk   70
2.1	Information Security Management System (ISMS) overview		70
2.2	How FAIR plugs into the ISMS		72
2.3	Major differences in approach		76
2.4	Recommended approach		78
2.5	Points to consider		78
	2.5.1	Concerns about the complexity of the model	78
	2.5.2	Availability of data to support statistical analysis	79
	2.5.3	The iterative nature of risk analyses	79

Chapter 3 What information is necessary for risk analysis?   80
3.1   Introduction to the landscape of risk 80
3.2   Asset landscape 80
        3.2.1   ISO definition and goal... 81
        3.2.2   Major differences in asset landscape treatment 82
3.3   Threat landscape 82
        3.3.1   ISO definition and goal... 82
        3.3.2   Major differences in threat landscape treatment 82
        3.3.3   Structure of classification 82
        3.3.4   Consideration of threat actions 83
        3.3.5   The development of metrics for the threat landscape 83
3.4   Controls landscape 84
        3.4.1   ISO definition and goal... 84
        3.4.2   Major differences in controls landscape treatment 84
        3.4.3   Development of metrics for the controls landscape 84
3.5   Loss (impact) landscape 85
        3.5.1   ISO definition and goal... 85
        3.5.2   Major differences in loss (impact) landscape treatment 85
        3.5.3   Structure of classification 85
        3.5.4   Development of metrics for the loss (impact) landscape 86
        3.5.5   Probability of indirect operational impacts 86
3.6   Vulnerability landscape 87
        3.6.1   ISO definition and goal... 87
        3.6.2   Major differences in vulnerability landscape treatment 87
        3.6.3   Consideration for the vulnerability landscape 87
        3.6.4   Development of metrics for the vulnerability landscape 88

Chapter 4 How to use FAIR in your ISMS   89
4.1   Recipe for ISO/IEC 27005 risk management with FAIR 90
4.2   Define the context for information security risk management 93
        4.2.1   General considerations 93
        4.2.2   Risk acceptance criteria 94
4.3   Calculate risk 95
        4.3.1   Stage 1 95
        4.3.2   Stage 2 96
        4.3.3   Stage 3 99
        4.3.4   Stage 4 100

4.4	Determine the appropriate information risk treatment plan	101
4.5	Develop an information security risk communication plan	102
4.6	Describe the information security risk monitoring and review plan	103

Appendix A Risk Management Program Worksheet 104

A.1	Define the context for information security risk management	104
A.2	Calculate risk	105
A.3	Determine the appropriate information risk treatment plan	108
A.4	Develop an Information Security Risk Communication Plan	109
A.5	Describe the Information Security Risk Monitoring and Review Plan	110

Glossary 111
Index 115

Introduction

This book brings together a set of three publications addressing risk management, which have been developed and approved by The Open Group. It is presented in three parts:
- Part 1: The Open Group Technical Standard for Risk Taxonomy
- Part 2: The Open Group Technical Guide to the Requirements for Risk Assessment Methodologies
- Part 3: The Open Group Technical Guide: FAIR – ISO/IEC 27005 Cookbook

Part 1: The Open Group Technical Standard for Risk Taxonomy
This part provides a standard definition and taxonomy for information security risk, as well as information regarding how to use the taxonomy.

The intended audience for this part includes anyone who needs to understand and/or analyze a risk condition. This includes, but is not limited to:
- Information security and risk management professionals
- Auditors and regulators
- Technology professionals
- Management

Note that this taxonomy is not limited to application in the information security space. It can, in fact, be applied to any risk scenario. This agnostic characteristic enables the taxonomy to be used as a foundation for normalizing the results of risk analyses across varied risk domains.

Part 2: The Open Group Technical Guide to the Requirements for Risk Assessment Methodologies
This part identifies and describes the key characteristics that make up any effective risk assessment methodology, thus providing a common set of criteria for evaluating any given risk assessment methodology against a clearly defined common set of essential requirements. In this way, it explains what features to look for when evaluating the capabilities of any given methodology, and the value those features represent.

The intended audience for this part is anyone who is tasked with selecting, performing, evaluating, or developing a risk assessment methodology. This includes all stakeholders who have responsibilities covering these areas, including business managers, information security/risk management professionals, auditors, and regulators both acting as policy-makers and as law-makers.

Part 3: The Open Group Technical Guide: FAIR – ISO/IEC 27005 Cookbook
This part describes in detail how to apply the FAIR (Factor Analysis for Information Risk) methodology to any selected risk management framework. It uses ISO/IEC 27005 as the example risk assessment framework. FAIR is complementary to all other risk assessment models/frameworks, including COSO, ITIL, ISO/IEC 27002, COBIT, OCTAVE, etc. It provides an engine that can be used in other risk models to improve the quality of the risk assessment results. The Cookbook enables risk technology practitioners to follow by example how to apply FAIR to other risk assessment models/frameworks of their choice.

The primary target audience for this Cookbook is risk management analysts and practitioners, to help them to use ISO/IEC 27005 to achieve higher quality risk assessment results, especially given the lack of formal specificity in probabilism provided by ISO/IEC 27005, including its difficult appendices on creation of a probabilistic model.

PART 1 THE OPEN GROUP TECHNICAL STANDARD

Risk Taxonomy

Chapter 1 Introduction to risk taxonomy 2
Chapter 2 Business case for a risk taxonomy 7
Chapter 3 Risk management model 12
Chapter 4 Functional aspects 13
Chapter 5 Technical aspects 14
Chapter 6 Example application 31
Appendix A Risk taxonomy considerations 43

Chapter 1 Introduction to risk taxonomy

1.1 Scope

This Technical Standard provides a taxonomy describing the factors that drive risk – their definitions and relationships.

This Technical Standard is not a reference or tutorial on how to assess or analyze risk, as there are many such references already available. This Technical Standard also does not cover those elements of risk management that pertain to strategic and tactical risk decisions and execution.

In the overall context of risk management, it is important to appreciate that our business objective in performing risk assessments is to identify and estimate levels of exposure to the likelihood of loss, so that business managers can make informed business decisions on how to manage those risks of loss – either by accepting each risk, or by mitigating it – through investing in appropriate internal protective measures judged sufficient to lower the potential loss to an acceptable level, or by investing in external indemnity. Critical to enabling good business decision-making therefore is to use risk assessment methods which give objective, meaningful, consistent results.

Fundamental to risk assessments is a sound approach:
You can't effectively and consistently manage what you can't measure, and you can't measure what you haven't defined.

The problem here is that a variety of definitions do exist, but the risk management community has not yet adopted a consistent definition for even the most fundamental terms in its vocabulary; e.g., threat, vulnerability, even risk itself. Without a sound common understanding of what risk is, what the factors are that drive risk, and a standard use of the terms we use to describe it, we can't be effective in delivering meaningful, comparable risk assessment results. This Risk Taxonomy provides the necessary foundation vocabulary, based on a fundamental analysis of what risk is, and then shows how to apply it to produce the objective, meaningful, and consistent results that business managers need.

1.2 Purpose/objective

The purpose and objective of this Technical Standard is to provide a single logical and rational taxonomical framework for anyone who needs to understand and/or analyze information security risk. It can and should be used to:

- Educate information security, risk, and audit professionals
- Establish a common language for the information security and risk management profession
- Introduce rigor and consistency into analysis, which sets the stage for more effective risk modeling
- Explain the basis for risk analysis conclusions
- Strengthen existing risk assessment and analysis methods
- Create new risk assessment and analysis methods
- Evaluate the efficacy of risk assessment and analysis methods
- Establish metric standards and data sources

1.3 Context

Although the terms "risk" and "risk management" mean different things to different people, this Technical Standard is intended to be applied toward the problem of managing the frequency and magnitude of loss that arises from a threat (whether human, animal, or natural event). In other words, managing "how often bad things happen, and how bad they are when they occur".

Although the concepts and taxonomy within this Technical Standard were not developed with the intention of being applied towards other risk types, experience has demonstrated that they can be effectively applied to other risk types. For example, they have been successfully applied in managing the likelihood and consequence of adverse events associated with project management or finance, in legal risk, and by statistical consultants in cases where probable impact is a concern (e.g., introducing a non-native species into an ecosystem).

1.4 The risk language gap

Over time, the ways we manage risk have evolved to keep up with the ways we conduct business. There is a very long history here, pre-dating the use of IT in business. As the scope, scale, and value of business operations have evolved, our specializations to manage the risk have similarly evolved, but in doing so each specialization has developed its own view of risk and how to describe its components. This has resulted in a significant language gap between the different specializations, all of whom are stakeholders in managing risk.

This gap is particularly evident between business managers and their IT risk/security specialists/analysts. For example, business managers talk about "impact" of loss, not in terms of how many servers or operational IT systems will cease to provide normal service, but rather what will be the impact of losing these normal services on the business's capacity to continue to trade normally, measured in terms of $-value; or whether the impact will be a failure to satisfy applicable regulatory requirements, which could force them to limit or even cease trading and perhaps become liable to heavy legal penalties.

So, a business manager tends to think of a "threat" as something which could result in a loss which the business cannot absorb without seriously damaging its trading position. Compare this with our Risk Taxonomy definitions for "threat" and "vulnerability":

Threat   Anything that is capable of acting in a manner resulting in harm to an asset and/or organization; for example, acts of God (weather, geological events, etc.); malicious actors; errors; failures.

Vulnerability   The probability that threat capability exceeds the ability to resist the threat.

Similar language gaps exist between other stakeholders in management of risk. Politicians and lawyers are particularly influential stakeholders. They are in the powerful position of shaping national and international policy (e.g., OECD, European Commission) which in turn influences national governments to pass laws and regulatory regimes on business practices that become effective one to three years down the line.

This Risk Taxonomy is an essential step towards enabling all stakeholders in risk management to use key risk management terms – especially Control, Asset, Threat, and Vulnerability – with precise meanings so we can bridge the language gap between IT specialists, business managers, lawyers, politicians, and other professionals, in all sectors of industry and commerce and the critical infrastructure, whose responsibilities bear on managing risk.

1.5 Using FAIR with other risk assessment frameworks

As The Open Group seeks to further its risk management framework based on FAIR (Factor Analysis for Information Risk), it is important to understand what the strengths of a FAIR approach are, and how they complement the work of other standards bodies. This section explains the outputs of a FAIR analysis and how these outputs are valuable in augmenting other risk assessment frameworks.

A valuable starting point here is the work published by the European Network and Information Security Agency (ENISA) in its November 2007 paper: Methods for the identification of Emerging and Future Risks. This ENISA document described how 18 various risk assessment frameworks addressed the criteria that the agency thought were important in assessing risk, and graded them on a numerical scale. In reviewing ENISA's criteria, the rating they assigned to each one, and the other risk assessment frameworks they reviewed, it became obvious that FAIR is not in direct competition with the other risk assessment frameworks, but actually is complementary to many of them.

1.5.1 The ability of a FAIR-based approach to complement other standards

FAIR, as a taxonomy of the factors that contribute to risk and how they affect each other, is primarily concerned with establishing accurate probabilities for the frequency and magnitude of loss events. It is not, *per se*, a "cookbook" that describes how to perform an enterprise (or individual) risk assessment. For example, FAIR documentation isn't so much concerned about the where and how you should get prior information for use in the assessment, as much as explaining how to describe the value of that information and how it contributes to creating risk.

So many risk assessment methodologies don't focus or concern themselves with how to establish consistent, defensible belief statements about risk – they simply give you steps they believe an organization should perform in order to have information for use in the creation of risk statements. FAIR can be used within the context of many of these standards without significant modifications to FAIR or the other methodology.

1.5.2 An example: using FAIR with OCTAVE

One good example might be using FAIR to augment an OCTAVE (Operationally Critical Threat, Asset, and Vulnerability Evaluation) assessment. OCTAVE is a risk assessment methodology developed and sold by US-CERT (refer to www.cert.org/octave). In Version 2 of the OCTAVE criteria, the document authors mention at least three times that: "Using probability … is optional". Section 3.2 of OCTAVE then directs assessors to establish their own criteria and context for developing values (high, medium, low) for "impact" and "likelihood". Unfortunately, OCTAVE gives no structured means to determine why likelihood might be "high" or why impact might be "low". OCTAVE simply states:

"It is important to establish criteria (for the qualitative expressions) that are meaningful to the organization."

Practitioners who want a means to develop "meaningful" risk statements using FAIR would simply use the FAIR taxonomy and framework to build consistent and defensible risk statements. This could be accomplished by augmenting Section 3 of the OCTAVE criteria with the relevant parts of the FAIR basic risk assessment methodology (see Chapter 1.6) which describes how FAIR's basic risk assessment methodology comprises ten steps in four stages. In this example, the risk criteria in Section 3.2 of the OCTAVE criteria would be strengthened by using the appropriate steps in the FAIR basic risk assessment methodology, and the statement of risk required by Section 3.3 of the OCTAVE criteria would similarly be able to use the appropriate step in the FAIR methodology.

1.5.3 Conclusion

Just by glancing through the relevant parts of the ENISA document, an experienced FAIR practitioner can identify several other methodologies that FAIR complements (NIST 800-30, ISO/IEC 27002:2005, COBIT, ITIL, for example). FAIR also complements risk assessment frameworks not included in the ENISA document (for example, COSO; refer to www.coso.org/-ERM.htm). In fact, there are no commonly used methodologies for performing or communicating risk that would be antagonistic to the use of FAIR.

As a standards body, The Open Group aims to evangelize the use of FAIR within the context of these risk assessment or management frameworks. In doing so, The Open Group becomes not just a group offering yet another risk assessment framework, but a standards body which solves the difficult problem of developing consistent, defensible statements concerning risk.

Chapter 2 Business case for a risk taxonomy

Risk management is fundamentally about making decisions – decisions about which risk issues are most critical (prioritization), which risk issues are not worth worrying about (risk acceptance), and how much to spend on the risk issues that need to be dealt with (budgeting). In order to be consistently effective in making these decisions, we need to be able to compare the issues themselves, as well as the options and solutions that are available. In order to compare, we need to measure, and measurement is predicated upon a solid definition of the things to be measured. Figure 2.1 shows these chained dependencies.

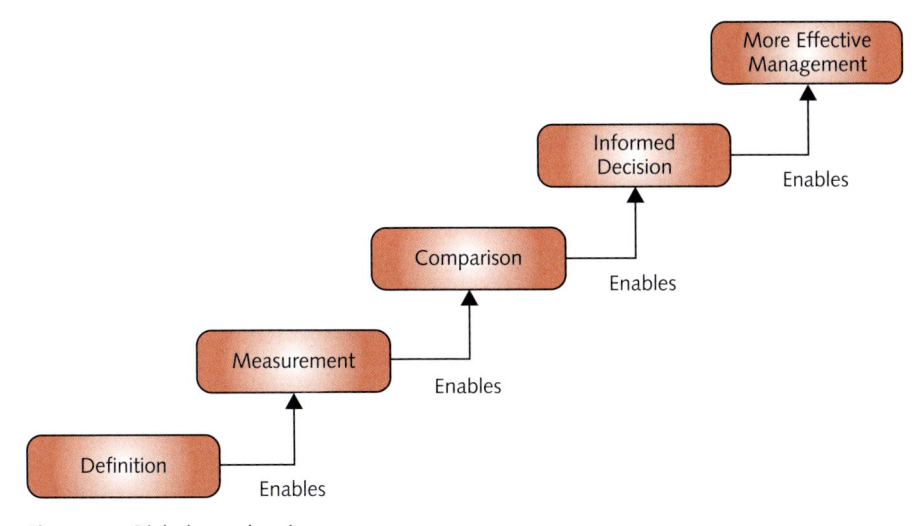

Figure 2.1: Risk dependencies

To date, the information security profession has been hamstrung by several challenges, not the least of which is inconsistent nomenclature. For example, in some references, software flaws/faults that could be exploited will be called a "threat", while in other references these same software faults will be referred to as a "risk", and yet other references will refer to them as "vulnerabilities". Besides the confusion that can result, this inconsistency makes it difficult if not impossible to normalize data and develop good metrics.

A related challenge stems from mathematical equations for risk that are either incomplete or illogical. For example, one commonly cited equation for risk states that:

*Risk = (Threat * Vulnerability) / Controls*

Amongst other problems, this equation doesn't tell us whether *Threat* means the level of force being applied or the frequency with which threat events occur. Furthermore, impact (magnitude of loss) is left out of the equation altogether. As we will touch on shortly, organization management cares very deeply about the question of loss magnitude, and so any risk equation that ignores impact is going to be meaningless to the very people who need to use risk analyses to make risk decisions.

These issues have been a major contributor to why the information security profession has consistently been challenged to find and maintain "a seat at the table" with the other organizational functions (e.g., finance, marketing, etc.). Furthermore, while few people are likely to become excited with the prospect of yet another set of definitions amongst the many that already exist, the capabilities that result from a well-designed foundational taxonomy are significant.

Likewise, in order for our profession to evolve significantly, it is imperative that we operate with a common, logical, and effective understanding of our fundamental problem space. This Risk Taxonomy Technical Standard seeks to fill the current void and set the stage for the security profession's maturation and growth.

Note: Any attempt to describe the natural world is destined to be incomplete and imprecise to some degree due to the simple fact that human understanding of the world is, and always will be, limited. Furthermore, the act of breaking down and categorizing a complex problem requires that black and white lines are drawn where, in reality, the world tends to be shades of gray. Nonetheless, this is exactly what human-critical analysis methods and science have done for millennia, resulting in a vastly improved ability to understand the world around us, evolve, and accomplish objectives previously believed to be unattainable.

This Technical Standard is a current effort at providing the foundational understanding that is necessary for similar evolution and accomplishment in managing information risk. Without this foundation, our profession will continue to rely too heavily on practitioner intuition which, although critically important, is often strongly affected by bias, myth, and commercial or personal agenda.

2.1 What makes this the standard of choice?

Although definitions and taxonomies already exist within the information security landscape, none provide a clear and logical representation of the fundamental problem our profession is tasked with managing – the frequency and magnitude of loss. For example:

- Existing taxonomies tend to focus on a subcomponent of the problem. Two current examples of work limited to particular areas of concern are the Common Weakness Enumeration (CWE) and the Common Attack Pattern Enumeration and Categorization (CAPEC).[1] However, while these two efforts are noteworthy, valuable, and consistent, most efforts are not consistent. In the absence of a common foundation it becomes difficult or impossible to tie together or interlink sub-taxonomies, which limits their utility to only the most narrow applications.
- Taxonomies are inconsistent in their use of common terms (e.g., "risk" in one taxonomy may translate to "vulnerability" in another). This makes normalization of data difficult, if not impossible, and leads to confusion and ineffective communication, which can further erode credibility.
- Documents that claim to describe "taxonomies" in fact provide definitions without clear descriptions (or, in some cases, without any descriptions) of the relationships between elements. Where information about these relationships is absent, it becomes impossible to perform meaningful calculations even when good data is available.

The risk taxonomy described within this Technical Standard provides several clear advantages over existing definitions and taxonomies, including:

- There is a clear focus on the problem that management cares about – the frequency and magnitude of loss.
- Risk factor definitions are conceptually consistent with other (non-security) risk concepts that organization management is already familiar with.
- It enables quantitative analysis of risk through the use of empirical data (where it exists) and/or subject matter expert estimates.
- It promotes consistent analyses between different analysts and analysis methods.
- It provides a framework for describing how risk conclusions were arrived at.

---

[1] Information about CWE is available at http://cwe.mitre.org, and information about CAPEC is available at http://capec.mitre.org.

- It effectively codifies the understanding of risk that many highly experienced professionals intuitively operate from but haven't had a reference for.
- It provides a reference and foundation for the evolution of specific sub-taxonomies.
- The multiple layers of abstraction within the model enable analysts to choose how deep/comprehensive they want to be in their analyses. This feature allows analysts to model risk in a cost-effective manner.

2.2 Who should use this Technical Standard?

This Technical Standard should be used by anyone seeking to:
- Understand how risk works and/or the factors that drive risk
- Consistently perform high quality risk analyses
- Develop or apply security metrics
- Evaluate, debate, or discuss the basis for risk conclusions
- Develop or apply risk analysis and assessment methodologies

A few examples of how the taxonomy can provide value are:
- Security organizations sometimes find that management rejects their risk conclusions and recommendations, in part because it's difficult to articulate the intuition and experience that led to those conclusions. The ability to explain how conclusions were arrived at using a logical and rigorous method can have a very significant impact on credibility in the eyes of management.
- Organizations often find that the quality and consistency of analyses performed by their security analysts vary widely. The Risk Taxonomy Technical Standard can be used to improve this by bringing everyone onto the same page with regard to terminology, definitions, and approach. This is especially helpful when bringing on staff who are newer to the profession, as it shortens the time it takes to make them effective.
- Metrics development and application are also improved by using the taxonomy to identify which data points are needed in order to support analyses, as well as where to get that data and how to use it. For example, data regarding threat contact frequency, the type of actions taken, which controls worked or failed to work, types and magnitude of loss, etc., can be extracted from incidents of all kinds (e.g., virus events, user errors, breaches, etc.) and used to support analyses.
- Organizations often engage external consultants to provide an impartial view of the organization's attitude to risk. The taxonomy can be used

very effectively to evaluate the consultants' risk conclusions and recommendations, ensuring that findings aren't inflated (or underrated). This ability to more consistently and effectively analyze risk is a critical factor in enabling more cost-effective risk management.

2.3 Related dependencies

In order to make effective use of this Technical Standard, risk assessment and analysis methodologies must provide data and/or estimates for each of the factors within the taxonomy. For example, if an assessment methodology leaves out or ignores threat event frequency, then conclusions resulting from the methodology will not align with the taxonomy, nor will they faithfully represent risk.

Note that where empirical data doesn't exist for one or more of the risk factors, it is acceptable to use subject matter expert estimates. For practical purposes, quantitative estimates should not be precise. Instead, estimates should be provided as ranges (e.g., "a threat event frequency of 1 to 10 times per year") or as distributions (e.g., "minimum 1 time per year, most likely 7 times per year, with a maximum of 10 times per year") with some form of confidence rating that represents the level of certainty surrounding the estimates.

If qualitative estimates are used as inputs (e.g., "high", "medium", "low"), the estimates should ideally be mapped to a predefined set of quantitative ranges (e.g., "Medium = 1 to 10"). This enables the relationships between factors within the taxonomy to be represented mathematically, which enables more effective risk calculation. It also provides a means for comparison between analyses performed by different analysts (normalization), as well as a means of explaining how conclusions were arrived at.

If pure qualitative values are used (i.e., values that don't reference a quantitative range or distribution), then the taxonomy may be used as a structural reference rather than a framework for calculation.

Note that the decision to use qualitative or quantitative values should be driven by the needs and desires of those who will receive or base their decisions on the analysis results. A secondary factor that may drive this choice is whether the analyst is comfortable using quantitative estimates.

Chapter 3 Risk management model

3.1 Risk assessment approach

All risk assessment approaches should include:
- An effort to clearly identify and characterize the assets, threats, controls, and impact/loss elements at play within the risk scenario being assessed
- An understanding of the organizational context for the analysis; i.e., what is at stake from an organizational perspective, particularly with regard to the organization's leadership perspective
- Measurement and/or estimation of the various risk factors
- Calculation of risk
- Communication of the risk results to decision-makers in a form that is meaningful and useful

3.2 Why is a tightly-defined taxonomy critical?

As alluded to earlier, without a logical, tightly-defined taxonomy, risk assessment approaches will be significantly impaired by an inability to measure and/or estimate risk factor variables. This, in turn, means that management will not have the necessary information for making well-informed comparisons and choices, which will lead to inconsistent and often cost-ineffective risk management decisions.

Chapter 4 Functional aspects

4.1 What is defined?

This Technical Standard defines and describes the problem space our profession is tasked with helping to manage: i.e., risk. Each factor that drives risk is identified and defined. Furthermore, the relationships between factors are described so that mathematical functions can be defined and used to perform quantitative calculations.

4.2 What is in/out of scope and why?

This Technical Standard is limited to describing the factors that drive risk and their relationships to one another. Measurement scales and specific assessment methodologies are not included because there are a variety of possible approaches to those aspects of risk analysis, with some approaches being better suited than others to specific risk problems and analysis objectives.

4.3 How should it be used?

This risk taxonomy should be used as a foundational reference of the problem space our profession is tasked with helping to manage: i.e., risk. Based on this foundation, methods for analyzing, calculating, communicating about, and managing risk can be developed.

Note that analysts can choose to make their measurements and/or estimates at any level of abstraction within the taxonomy. For example, rather than measure Contact Frequency, the analyst could move up a layer of abstraction and instead measure Threat Event Frequency. This choice may be driven by the nature or volume of data that is available, or the time available to perform the analysis (i.e., analyses at deeper layers of abstraction take longer).

Chapter 5 Technical aspects

5.1 Risk taxonomy overview

The complete risk taxonomy is comprised of two main branches: Loss Event Frequency and Probable Loss Magnitude. Within those two branches are the factors that drive the occurrence and magnitude of losses. Figure 5.1 lays out the higher-level abstractions within the framework.

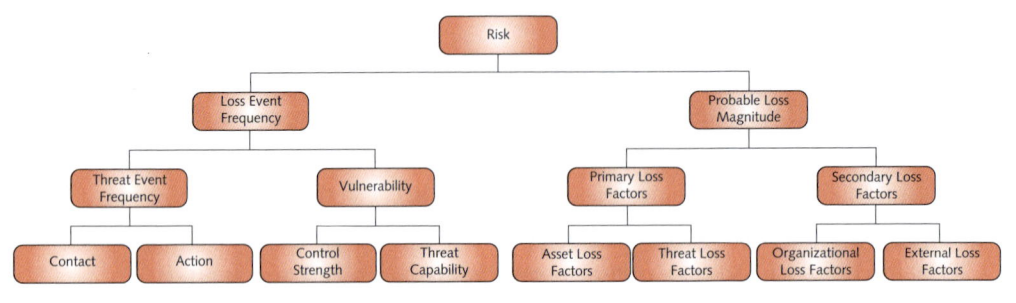

Figure 5.1: Risk taxonomy overview

Note that this diagram is not comprehensive, as deeper layers of abstraction exist that are not shown. Some of these deeper layers are discussed further on in this Technical Standard, but it is important to recognize that, theoretically, the layers of abstraction may continue indefinitely, much like the layers of abstraction that exist in our understanding of physical matter (e.g., molecules, atoms, particles, etc.). The deeper layers of abstraction can be useful in our understanding but generally aren't necessary in order to perform effective analyses.

Another point worth recognizing is that the factors within the Loss Event Frequency side of the taxonomy have relatively clean and clear cause-and-effect relationships with one another, which simplifies calculation. Factors within the Probable Loss Magnitude side of the taxonomy, however, have much more complicated relationships that defy simple calculation. As a result, loss magnitude measurements and estimates generally are aggregated by loss type (e.g., $xxx of productivity loss, plus $yyy of legal fines and judgments, etc.).

5.2 Component definitions

5.2.1 Risk

Risk is the probable frequency and probable magnitude of future loss. With this as a starting point, the first two obvious components of risk are loss frequency and loss magnitude. In this Technical Standard, these are referred to as Loss Event Frequency (LEF) and Probable Loss Magnitude (PLM), respectively. See Figure 5.2.

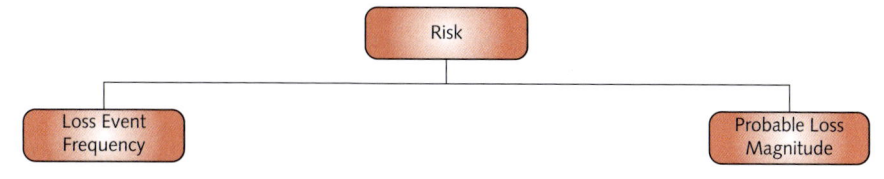

Figure 5.2: High level components of risk

We will decompose the factors that drive Loss Event Frequency first, and then examine the factors that drive Probable Loss Magnitude.

5.2.2 Loss Event Frequency (LEF)

Loss Event Frequency (LEF) is the occurrence, within a given timeframe, that a threat agent will inflict harm upon an asset.

In order for a loss event to occur, a threat agent has to act upon an asset, such that loss results. This leads us to our next two factors: Threat Event Frequency (TEF) and Vulnerability (Figure 5.3).

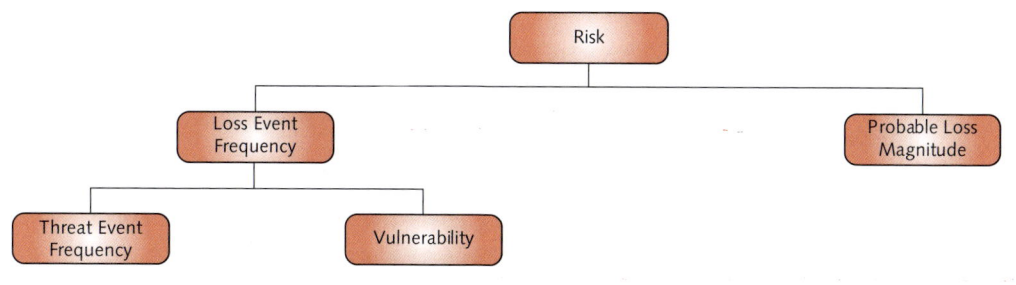

Figure 5.3: Loss Event Frequency

Note that time-framing is key to differentiating between possibility and probability because, given enough time, almost any event is possible. By using a short enough time-framing in our analysis, we are more or less forced to treat the issue as a probability.

5.2.3 Threat Event Frequency (TEF)

Threat Event Frequency (TEF) is the occurrence, within a given timeframe, that a threat agent will act against an asset.

You will probably see the similarity between this definition and the definition for LEF above. The only difference is that the definition for TEF doesn't include whether threat agent actions are successful. In other words, threat agents may act against assets, but be unsuccessful in affecting the asset. A common example would be the hacker who unsuccessfully attacks a web server. Such an attack would be considered a threat event, but not a loss event.

This definition also provides us with the two factors that drive Threat Event Frequency: Contact and Action. Note that Action is predicated upon Contact. Figure 5.4 adds these two factors to our taxonomy.

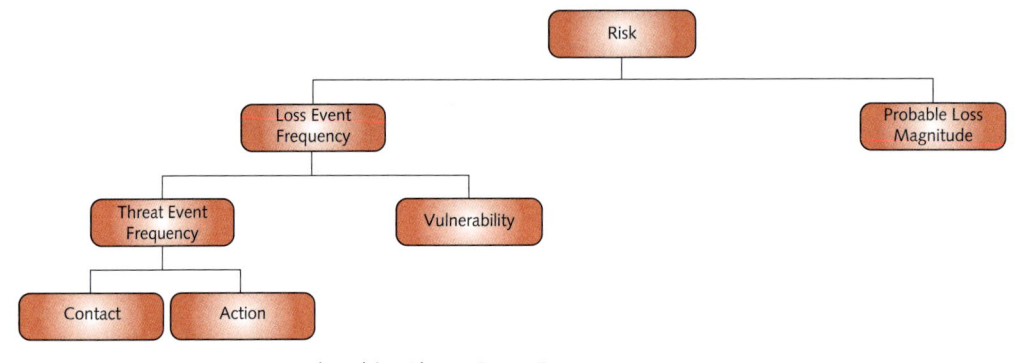

Figure 5.4: Factors that drive Threat Event Frequency

5.2.4 Contact

Contact is the probable frequency, within a given timeframe, that a threat agent will come into contact with an asset.

Contact can be physical or "logical" (e.g., over the network). Regardless of contact mode, three types of Contact can take place, as follows:
- Random – the threat agent "stumbles upon" the asset during the course of unfocused or undirected activity.
- Regular – contact occurs because of the regular actions of the threat agent. For example, if the cleaning crew regularly comes by at 5:15, leaving cash on top of the desk during that timeframe sets the stage for contact.
- Intentional – the threat agent seeks out specific targets.

Each of these types of Contact is driven by various factors. A useful analogy is to consider a container of fluid containing two types of suspended particles – threat particles and asset particles. The probability of contact between members of these two sets of particles is driven by various factors, including:
- Size (surface area) of the particles
- The number of particles
- Volume of the container
- How active the particles are
- Viscosity of the fluid
- Whether particles are attracted to one another in some fashion, etc.

5.2.5 Action

Action is the probability that a threat agent will act against an asset once Contact occurs.

Once Contact occurs between a threat agent and an asset, Action against the asset may or may not take place. For some threat agent types, Action always takes place. For example, if a tornado comes into contact with a house, action is a foregone conclusion. Action is only in question when we're talking about "thinking" threat agents such as humans and other animals, and artificially intelligent threat agents like malicious programs (which are extensions of their human creators) and where the opportunity for decision on causing alternative loss or no loss exists.

The probability that an intentional act will take place is driven by three primary factors, as follows:
- Value – the threat agent's perceived value proposition from performing the act.
- Level of effort – the threat agent's expectation of how much effort it will take to accomplish the act.
- Risk – the probability of negative consequences to the threat agent; for example, the probability of getting caught and suffering unacceptable consequences for acting maliciously.

5.2.6 Vulnerability

Having covered the high-level factors that drive whether threat events take place, we now turn our attention to the factors that drive whether the asset is able to resist threat agent actions.

Vulnerability is the probability that an asset will be unable to resist the actions of a threat agent.

Vulnerability exists when there is a difference between the force being applied by the threat agent, and an object's ability to resist that force. This simple analysis provides us with the two primary factors that drive vulnerability: Threat Capability and Control Strength (resistance capability). Figure 5.5 adds these factors to our taxonomy.

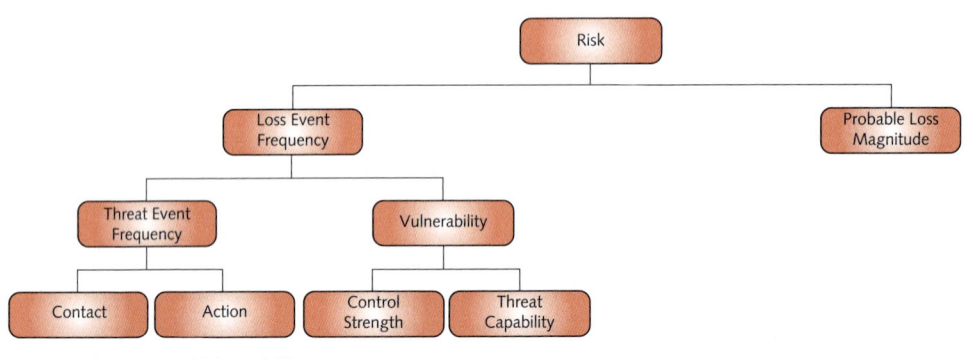

Figure 5.5: Vulnerability

Vulnerability is always relative to the type of force and vector involved. In other words, the tensile strength of a rope is pertinent only if the threat agent force is a weight applied along the length of the rope. Tensile strength doesn't generally apply to a scenario where the threat agent is fire, chemical erosion, etc. Likewise, a computer anti-virus product doesn't provide much in the way of protection from the internal employee seeking to perpetrate fraud. The key, then, is to evaluate vulnerability in the context of specific threat types and control types.

One final point regarding vulnerability: there's no such thing as being more than 100 percent vulnerable to damage by any specific threat agent/attack vector combination. Vulnerability can exist such that harm can occur from more than one threat agent through more than one attack vector, but each of those represents a different potential threat event. For example, if I'm walking down the street at night in a particularly dangerous part of town, I'm vulnerable to multiple potential threat events; for example, being run over by a car, being mugged, or being the victim of a drive-by shooting. My vulnerability to any one of these events cannot exceed 100 percent, yet my aggregate risk is obviously greater as a result of the multiple threat scenarios.

5.2.7 Threat Capability

Threat Capability is the probable capability a threat agent is capable of applying against an asset.

Not all threat agents are created equal. In fact, threat agents within a single threat community are not all going to have the same capabilities. What this should tell us is that the probability of the most capable threat agent acting against an asset is something less than 10 percent. In fact, depending upon the threat community under analysis, and other conditions within the scenario, the probability of encountering a highly capable threat agent may be remote.

As information security professionals, we often struggle with the notion of considering threat agent capability as a probability. We tend, instead, to gravitate toward focusing on the worst case. But if we look closely at the issue, it is clear that focusing solely on worst case is to think in terms of possibility rather than probability.

Another important consideration is that some threat agents may be very proficient in applying one type of force, and incompetent at others. For example, a network engineer is likely to be proficient at applying technological forms of attack, but may be relatively incapable of executing complex accounting fraud.

5.2.8 Control Strength (CS)

Control Strength (CS) is the strength of a control as compared to a baseline measure of force.

A rope's tensile strength rating provides an indication of how much force it is capable of resisting. The baseline measure (CS) for this rating is pounds per square inch (PSI), which is determined by the rope's design and construction. This CS rating doesn't change when the rope is put to use. Regardless of whether you have a 10-pound weight on the end of the 500-PSI rope, or a 2000-pound weight, the CS doesn't change.

Unfortunately, the information risk realm doesn't have a baseline scale for force that is as well defined as PSI. Consider, however, password strength as a simple example of how we can approach this. We can estimate that a password eight characters long, comprised of a mixture of upper and lowercase letters, numbers, and special characters, will resist the cracking attempts of some percentage of the *general threat agent population*. The password Control Strength (CS) can be represented as this percentage. (Recall that CS is relative to a particular type of force – in this case cracking.) Vulnerability is determined by comparing CS against the capability of the *specific threat community* under analysis. For example, password CS may be estimated at 8 percent, yet the threat community within a scenario might be estimated to have better than average capabilities – let's say in the 90 percent range. The difference represents Vulnerability.

5.2.9 Probable Loss Magnitude (PLM)

Probable Loss Magnitude (PLM) is the likely outcome of a threat event. The previous section introduced the factors that drive the probability of loss events occurring. This section describes the other half of the risk equation – the factors that drive loss magnitude when events occur.

Unfortunately, Probable Loss Magnitude (PLM) is one of the toughest nuts to crack in analyzing risk. Various approaches have been tried, with varying degrees of success, but none have gained widespread use or acceptance. As a result, we often exclude loss uncertainty considerations altogether; we only cite the worst-case possibilities, or we try to be precise in our calculations. Excluding loss-related uncertainties from an analysis means that we are not analyzing risk (by definition, risk *always* has a loss component). Citing worst-case possibilities alone removes the probability element from our analysis (by definition, risk is a probability issue). Trying to be precise is generally a waste of time because of the inherent complexity within loss, and because decision-makers generally only need a ballpark idea of the loss probabilities. Management's experience with other forms of risk (investment, market, etc.) has taught them that actual losses can't be predicted with any precision.

There are a number of reasons why it is difficult to evaluate loss probability; for example:
- It is very difficult to put a precise value on assets at risk.
- Assets generally have more than one value or liability characteristic.
- Loss can take many forms.
- A single event can result in more than one form of loss.
- Frequent events are easier to treat probabilistically; rare or novel ones are hard.

- Complex systemic relationships exist between the different forms of loss.
- Many factors determine loss magnitude.

Making matters even more difficult in the information risk environment is the fact that we have very little good data about loss magnitude. Many organizations don't perform loss analysis when events occur, and those that do track loss often limit their analyses to the "easy stuff" (e.g., person-hours, equipment replacement, etc.). Furthermore, without a standard taxonomy, it's very difficult to normalize the data across organizations.

Information security incidents generally have a distribution that looks something like Figure 5.6.

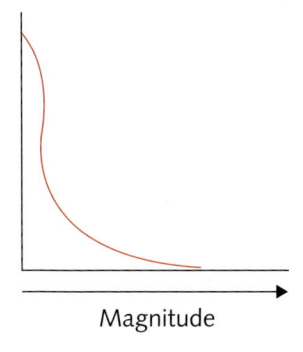

Figure 5.6: Distribution of information security incidents

There are far more events that result in loss at the low end of the magnitude spectrum than there are at the high end of the spectrum. For example, individual virus incidents, unauthorized use of systems to serve up MP3 files, even password cracking and web site defacement, rarely result in significant loss. The question we have to ask ourselves is "Why?". What factors are responsible for this? Clearly some of these events have significant potential for harm, but if we compared the *actual* loss from two similar events – one in which minimal loss occurred, and another where substantial loss occurred – what factors determined the difference? In order for us to make reasoned estimates of loss, we have to understand these factors.

5.2.10 Forms of loss

An asset's loss potential stems from the value it represents and/or the liability it introduces to an organization. For example, customer information provides value through its role in generating revenue for a commercial organization.

That same information can also introduce liability to the organization if a legal duty exists to protect it, or if customers have an expectation that the information about them will be appropriately protected.

Six forms of loss are defined within this Technical Standard, as follows:
- Productivity – the reduction in an organization's ability to generate its primary value proposition (e.g., income, goods, services, etc.).
- Response – expenses associated with managing a loss event (e.g., internal or external person-hours, logistical expenses, etc.).
- Replacement – the intrinsic value of an asset. Typically represented as the capital expense associated with replacing lost or damaged assets (e.g., rebuilding a facility, purchasing a replacement laptop, etc.).
- Fines and judgments (F/J) – legal or regulatory actions levied against an organization. Note that this includes bail for any organization members who are arrested.
- Competitive advantage (CA) – losses associated with diminished competitive advantage. Within this framework, CA loss is specifically associated with assets that provide competitive differentiation between the organization and its competition. Within the commercial world, examples would include trade secrets, merger and acquisition plans, etc. Outside the commercial world, examples would include military secrets, secret alliances, etc.
- Reputation – losses associated with an external perception that an organization's leadership is incompetent, criminal, or unethical.

Keep in mind that loss is evaluated from a single perspective – typically that of the organization under analysis. For example, although customers might be harmed if their personal information is stolen, our risk analysis would evaluate the losses experienced by the organization rather than the losses experienced by the customers.

5.2.11 Loss factors
All loss factors fall within one of the following four categories:
- Asset
- Threat
- Organization
- External

For reasons that will become clear, asset and threat loss factors are referred to as *primary loss factors*, while organizational and external loss factors are referred to as *secondary loss factors*. See Figure 5.7.

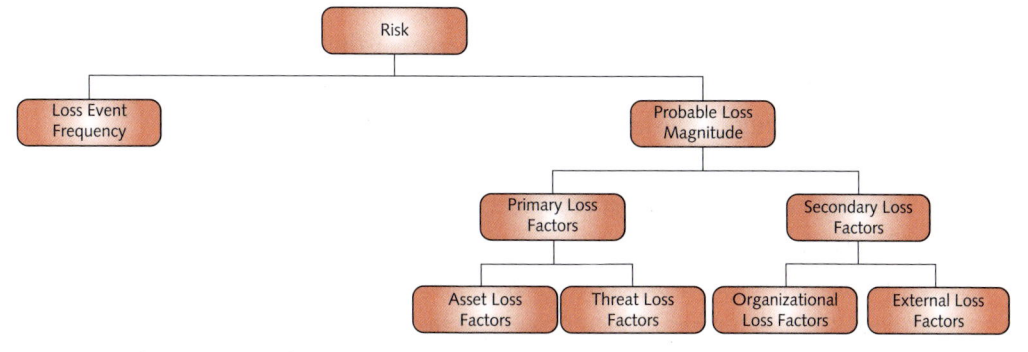

Figure 5.7: Loss factors

In order for us to make reasoned judgments about the form and magnitude of loss within any given scenario, we have to evaluate the factors within all four of these categories. Within this Technical Standard, we will limit our discussion to some of the most common and most important loss factors.

5.2.12 Primary loss factors

Asset loss factors

There are two asset loss factors that we are concerned with: value/liability and volume (Figure 5.8).

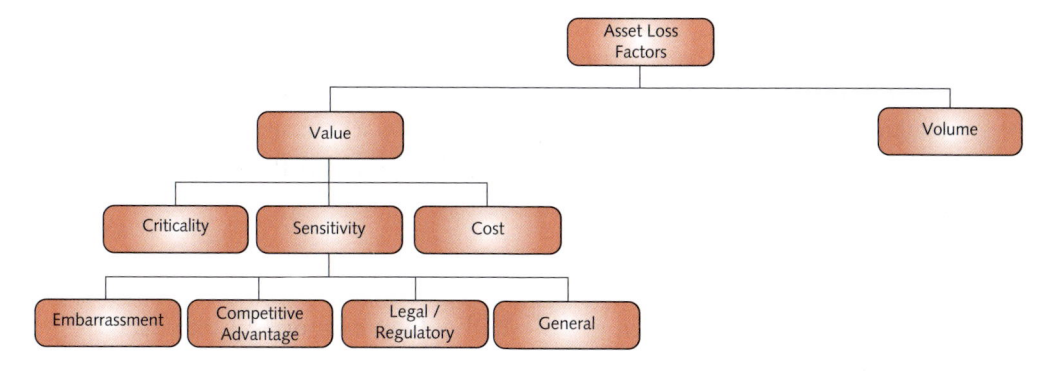

Figure 5.8: Asset loss factors

As alluded to above, and as we'll see when we cover measurement, the value/liability characteristics of an asset play a key role in both the nature and magnitude of loss. We can further define value/liability as:

- Criticality – characteristics of an asset that have to do with the impact to an organization's productivity. For example, the impact a corrupted database would have on the organization's ability to generate revenue.
- Cost – the intrinsic value of the asset; i.e., the cost associated with replacing it if it has been made unavailable (e.g., stolen, destroyed, etc.). Examples include the cost of replacing a stolen laptop or rebuilding a bombed-out building.
- Sensitivity – the harm that can occur from unintended disclosure. Sensitivity is further broken down into four sub-categories:
  - **Embarrassment/reputation** – the information provides evidence of incompetent, criminal, or unethical management. Note that this refers to reputation damage resulting from the nature of the information itself, as opposed to reputation damage that may result when a loss event takes place.
  - **Competitive advantage** – the information provides competitive advantage (e.g., key strategies, trade secrets, etc.). Of the sensitivity categories, this is the only one where the sensitivity represents value. In all other cases, sensitivity represents liability.
  - **Legal/regulatory** – the organization is bound by law to protect the information.
  - **General** – sensitive information that doesn't fall into any of the above categories, but would result in some form of loss if disclosed.

Asset volume simply recognizes that more assets at risk equals greater loss magnitude if an event occurs; e.g., two children on a rope swing *versus* one child, or one sensitive customer record *versus* a thousand.

Threat loss factors
Within this document, we'll limit our threat considerations to three threat loss factors: action, competence, and whether the threat agent is internal or external to the organization. See Figure 5.9.

Threat agents can take one or more of the following actions against an asset:
- Access – simple unauthorized access.
- Misuse – unauthorized use of assets (e.g., identity theft, setting up a pornographic distribution service on a compromised server, etc.).

```
                    Threat Loss
                     Factors
        ┌───────────────┼───────────────┐
   Competence         Action       Internal versus
                                      External
    ┌──────┬───────────┼───────────┬──────┐
  Access  Misuse    Disclose    Modify  Deny Access
```

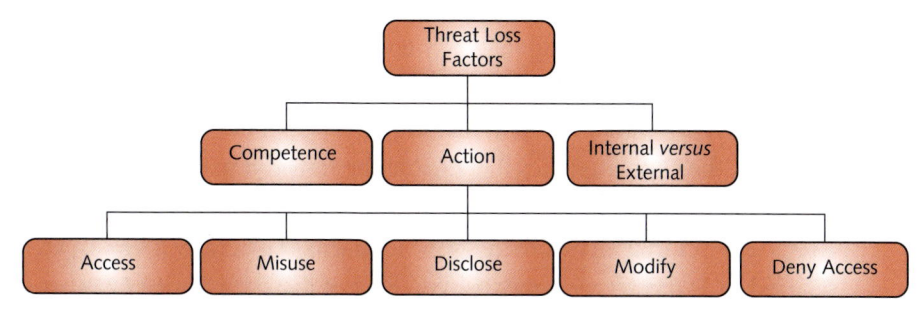

Figure 5.9: Threat loss factors

- Disclose – the threat agent illicitly discloses sensitive information.
- Modify – unauthorized changes to an asset.
- Deny access – includes destruction, theft of a non-data asset, etc.

It is important to recognize that each of these actions affects different assets differently, which drives the degree and nature of loss. For example, the potential for productivity loss resulting from a destroyed or stolen asset depends upon how critical that asset is to the organization's productivity. If a critical asset is simply illicitly accessed, there is no direct productivity loss. Similarly, the destruction of a highly sensitive asset that doesn't play a critical role in productivity won't directly result in a significant productivity loss. Yet that same asset, if disclosed, can result in significant loss of competitive advantage or reputation, and generate legal costs. The point is that it's the combination of the asset, kind of violation, and kind of exploitation of this violation that determines the fundamental nature and degree of loss.

Which action(s) a threat agent takes will be driven primarily by that agent's motive (e.g., financial gain, revenge, recreation, etc.) and the nature of the asset. For example, a threat agent bent on financial gain is less likely to destroy a critical server than they are to steal an easily pawned asset like a laptop. For this reason, it is critical to have a clear definition of your threat community in order to effectively evaluate loss magnitude.

This is similar to the Threat Capability factor that contributes to vulnerability. The difference is subtle, but important. Threat Competence has to do with the amount of damage a threat agent is capable of inflicting once the compromise occurs, while Threat Capability to Violate has to do with the threat agent's ability to put itself in a position to inflict harm. An example may help to clarify this point. A terrorist threat agent has capabilities they would employ in an attempt to access nuclear secrets. These capabilities play a role in the likelihood that they'll be successful in gaining access. Their ability to inflict harm once they've acquired the secrets (e.g., build a bomb) is, however, dependent upon a different set of competencies. In this Technical Standard, the characteristics that enable the terrorist to compromise defenses and be in a position to acquire the secrets are called *threat capabilities*. The characteristics that enable them to inflict harm (e.g., create a bomb) are referred to as *threat competencies*. We will not dwell on Threat Competence in this document. Nonetheless, it's useful to recognize that this factor exists in order to have a more complete understanding of risk.

The consideration of whether a threat agent is external or internal to the organization can play a pivotal role in how much loss occurs. Specifically, loss events generated by malicious internal threat agents (including employees, contractors, etc.) *typically* have not resulted in significant regulatory or reputation losses because it is recognized that trusted insiders are exceedingly difficult to protect against.

5.2.13 Secondary loss factors

Secondary loss factors are those organizational and external characteristics of the environment that influence the nature and degree of loss.

Organizational loss factors

There are many organizational loss factors. Within this document, we will limit our discussion to four – timing, due diligence, response, and detection.

- The timing of an event can have a tremendous impact on loss. For example, an event occurring in the midst of a big advertising campaign may create significantly greater loss than a similar event at some other time of year.
- Due diligence can play a significant role in the degree of liability an organization faces from an event. If reasonable preventative measures were not in place (given the threat environment and value of the asset), then legal and reputation damage can be far more severe. The challenge is that "reasonable preventative measures" are not universally defined or agreed upon. Often, "industry standards" or theoretical "best practices" are looked to as guidelines for due diligence. Unfortunately, these guidelines typically don't consider the threat environment or loss magnitude. Consequently, industry standards and best practices may be insufficient (i.e., not truly representative of due diligence) or overly conservative (i.e., prohibitively expensive given the real risk).

How effectively an organization *responds* to an event can spell the difference between an event nobody remembers a year later, and one that stands out as an example (good or bad) in the annals of history. There are three components to a response:

- Containment – an organization's ability to limit the breadth and depth of an event; for example, cordoning-off the network to contain the spread of a worm.
- Remediation – an organization's ability to remove the threat agent; e.g., eradicating the worm.
- Recovery – the ability to bring things back to normal.

All three of these response components must exist, and the degree to which any of them is deficient can have a significant impact on loss magnitude.

We tend to think of response capabilities solely within the context of criticality; i.e., the ability to return productivity to normal. It is critical to recognize, however, that response capabilities can also significantly affect losses resulting from sensitive information disclosure. For example, an organization that experiences a publicly disclosed breach of confidential customer information generally can significantly reduce its losses by being forthright in its admissions, and by fully compensating harmed parties. Conversely, an organization that denies and deflects responsibility is much more likely to become a pariah and a media whipping post.

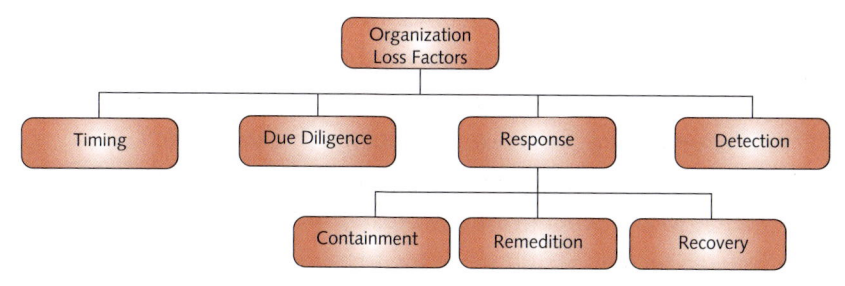

Figure 5.10: Organizational loss factors

You can't respond to something you haven't detected; i.e., response is predicated on detection. In training sessions, the question often comes up: "What about those events we may not know about – the corporate spies, etc.?" Clearly, incidents take place that don't show up on the radar. However, it's also reasonable to believe that such events – if they result in material loss – will almost always be detected eventually. For example, the damage from sensitive competitive advantage information that makes its way to a competitor *will* materialize and almost certainly be recognized. Was the detection timely? Perhaps not. However, once detected, the organization may still have an opportunity to respond and reduce its losses. For example, legal action against a competitor who stole proprietary information might be appropriate. The point is that material loss is almost certain to be detected, and with detection comes an opportunity to respond and manage loss magnitude.

External loss factors
External loss factors generally fall into one of the following five categories – detection, the legal and regulatory landscape, the competitive landscape, the media, and external stakeholders (e.g., customers, partners, stockholders, etc.).

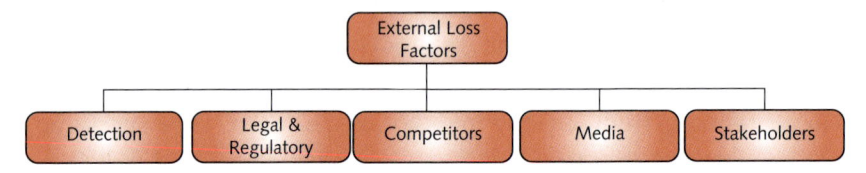

Figure 5.11: External loss factors

A couple of important things to recognize about external loss factors include:
- These four categories represent entities that can inflict a secondary form of harm upon the organization as a consequence of an event. In other words, events will often result in direct forms of loss (e.g., productivity, response, replacement) due to the criticality and inherent value characteristics of assets. Secondary losses may also occur based upon the external reaction to a loss event (e.g., sensitive information disclosure, etc.).
- All of the factors within these external categories can be described as "reactive to an event". In other words, in order for an external factor to affect loss magnitude, the event has to be detected by an external entity. For example, if an employee executes identity theft by misusing their legitimate access to customer information, the customer(s), regulators, and lawyers can't inflict harm upon the organization unless the identity theft is tied back to the organization. Likewise, if a productivity outage occurs but isn't detected by customers, partners, etc., then the organization will not be subject to a negative response on the part of those stakeholders.

This last point leads us to our first external loss factor – *detection*. Based upon the premise above, we can think of detection as a binary factor on which all other external factors are predicated. External detection of an event can happen as a consequence of the severity of the event, through intentional actions by the threat agent, through unauthorized disclosure by someone on the inside who's familiar with the event, intentional disclosure by the organization (either out of sense of duty, or because it is required by law), or by accident.

The legal and regulatory landscape is primarily made up of three parts – regulations (local, state, federal, and international), contract law, and case law. Although this component of the external landscape is evolving rapidly, it is safe to say that fines and sanctions can be significant for organizations within regulated industries. In theory, however, fines and judgments are driven in part by how much harm actually occurs from an event and the level of due diligence exercised to prevent it from occurring in the first place. In other words, if an event occurs that represents a regulatory or legal breach, fines and judgments should reflect how much harm actually occurs to the affected stakeholders as well as how proactive the organization was in preventing the loss.

Losses associated with the competitive landscape typically have to do with the competition's ability to take advantage of the situation. For example, if an organization experiences an event that causes its stakeholders to consider taking their business elsewhere, a competitor's ability to leverage that weakness will affect how much loss occurs.

Media reaction can have a powerful affect on how stakeholders, lawyers, and even regulators and competitors view the event. If the media chooses to vilify the organization, and keep it on the headlines for an extended period, the result can be devastating. Conversely, if the media paints the organization as a well-intentioned victim who exercised due diligence but still suffered the event at the hands of a criminal, then legal and reputation damage can be minimized. This is why organizations *must* have effective crisis communication processes in place.

External stakeholders generally inflict harm by taking their business elsewhere; i.e., supporting a rival. This happens when they:
- Have been harmed directly as a result of an incident. The organization's response to the event is crucial in mitigating this exposure.
- Perceive that their interests are better served elsewhere (the organization's value proposition is diminished). Here again, an organization generally has some opportunity to mitigate this exposure through prompt, effective action.
- View the organization (or, more accurately, its leadership) as incompetent, untrustworthy, and/or criminal. This can be a much tougher exposure to mitigate.

Chapter 6 Example application

This chapter provides an example of how the taxonomy may be used to perform a risk analysis. The analysis steps and charts shown are borrowed from the Introduction to Factor Analysis of Information Risk (FAIR). Note that any other well-designed analysis method could be used instead.

6.1 The scenario

A Human Resources (HR) executive within a large bank has his username and password written on a sticky-note stuck to his computer monitor. These authentication credentials allow him to log onto the network and access the HR applications he is entitled to use.

Before we get started, think to yourself how you would rate the level of risk within this scenario based upon the assessments you've seen or done in the past.

6.2 The analysis: FAIR basic risk assessment methodology

The simplified process we'll use in this example is comprised of ten steps in four stages, as follows:
- Stage 1: Identify scenario components:
  - Identify the asset at risk
  - Identify the threat community under consideration
- Stage 2: Evaluate Loss Event Frequency (LEF):
  - Estimate the probable Threat Event Frequency (TEF)
  - Estimate the Threat Capability (TCap)
  - Estimate Control Strength (CS)
  - Derive Vulnerability (Vuln)
  - Derive Loss Event Frequency (LEF)
- Stage 3: Evaluate Probable Loss Magnitude (PLM):
  - Estimate worst-case loss
  - Estimate Probable Loss Magnitude (PLM)
- Stage 4: Derive and articulate risk:
  - Derive and articulate risk

6.2.1 Stage 1: Identify scenario components

Identify the asset at risk

The first question we have to answer is: "What asset is at risk?" Another way to think about this is to determine where value or liability exists. A typical question in this scenario is whether the credentials are the asset, or whether it's the applications, systems, and information that the credentials provide access to. The short answer is "they're all assets". In this case, however, we'll focus on the credentials, recognizing that their value is inherited from the assets they are intended to protect.

Identify the threat community

The second question we have to answer is: "Risk associated with what threat?" If we examine the nature of the organization (e.g., the industry it's in, etc.), and the conditions surrounding the asset (e.g., an HR executive's office), we can begin to parse the overall threat population into communities that might reasonably apply. How many threat communities we choose to analyze, and how we subdivide them, is up to us. It's probably not a good use of time to include every conceivable threat community in our analysis. For example, given this scenario, it probably wouldn't be worthwhile to analyze the risk associated with nation-state intelligence services such as the French DGSE. Are we saying that it's not possible for a nation-state spy to attack this bank through this exposure? No. But by considering the nature of the threat communities relative to the industry, organization, and asset, we can come to reasonable conclusions without falling victim to analysis paralysis or "lottery odds nit-picking".

Within this scenario, it seems reasonable to consider the risk associated with the following threat communities:
- The cleaning crew
- Other HR workers with regular access to the executive's office
- Visitors to his office
- Guests
- Job applicants
- Technical support staff

With experience it becomes easier to determine which communities are worthwhile to include and exclude, and whether it makes sense to combine communities such as those that fall under "Visitors". For this example, we'll focus on the cleaning crew.

6.2.2 Stage 2: Evaluate Loss Event Frequency (LEF)

Estimate the probable Threat Event Frequency (TEF)
Many people demand reams of hard data before they are comfortable with estimating attack frequency. Unfortunately, because we don't have much (if any) really useful or credible data for many scenarios, TEF is often ignored altogether. The minute we ignore this component of risk, however, we are no longer talking about risk. So, in the absence of hard data, what's left? One answer is to use a qualitative scale, such as Low, Medium, or High. And, while there's nothing inherently wrong with a qualitative approach in many circumstances, a quantitative approach provides better clarity and is more useful to most decision-makers – *even if it's imprecise*. For example, I may not have years of empirical data documenting how frequently cleaning crew employees abuse usernames and passwords on sticky-notes, but I can make a reasonable estimate within a set of ranges.

A TEF estimate would be based upon how frequently contact between this threat community (the cleaning crew) and the credentials occurs *and* the probability that they would act against the credentials. If the cleaning crew comes by once per workday, contact reasonably occurs a couple of hundred times per year. The probability that they would act is driven by three primary factors:
- The value of the asset to them (based upon their motives – financial gain, revenge, etc.)
- How vulnerable the asset appears to be …
- versus the risk of being caught and suffering unacceptable consequences

Recognizing that cleaning crews are generally comprised of honest people, that an HR executive's credentials typically would not be viewed or recognized as especially valuable to them, and that the perceived risk associated with illicit use might be high, then it seems reasonable to estimate a Low TEF using Table 6.1 below.

Rating	Description
Very High (VH)	→ 100 times per year
High (H)	Between 10 and 100 times per year
Moderate (M)	Between 1 and 10 times per year
Low (L)	Between 0.1 and 1 times per year
Very Low (VL)	← 0.1 times per year (less than once every 10 years)

Table 6.1 Ratings for the values of Probable Threat Event Frequency

Is it possible for a cleaning crew to have an employee with motive, sufficient computing experience to recognize the potential value of these credentials, and with a high enough risk tolerance to try their hand at illicit use? Absolutely! Does it happen? Undoubtedly. Might such a person be on the crew that cleans this office? Sure – it's possible. Nonetheless, the probable frequency is relatively low.

Estimate the Threat Capability (TCap)

Threat Capability (Tcap) refers to the threat agent's skill (knowledge & experience) and resources (time & materials) that can be brought to bear against the asset. A different scenario might provide a better illustration of this component of the analysis – something like a web application with an SQL injection weakness – but scenarios like that don't lend themselves to an introductory document. In this case, all we're talking about here is estimating the skill (in this case, reading ability) and resources (time) the average member of this threat community can use against a password written on a sticky-note. It's reasonable to rate the cleaning crew Tcap as Medium, as compared to the overall threat population. Keep in mind that Tcap is always estimated relative to the scenario. If our scenario was different, and we were evaluating the cleaning crew's capability to execute an SQL injection attack, we'd probably rate them lower (see Table 6.2).

Rating	Description
Very High (VH)	Top 2% when compared against the overall threat population
High (H)	Top 16% when compared against the overall threat population
Moderate (M)	Average skill and resources (between bottom 16% and top 16%)
Low (L)	Bottom 16% when compared against the overall threat population
Very Low (VL)	Bottom 2% when compared against the overall threat population

Table 6.2 Ratings for the values of Threat Capability

Estimate Control Strength (CS)

Control Strength (CS) has to do with an asset's ability to resist compromise. In our scenario, because the credentials are in plain sight and in plain text, the CS is Very Low. If they were written down, but encrypted, the CS would be different – probably much higher (see Table 6.3).

Rating	Description
Very High (VH)	Protects against all but the top 2% of an average threat population
High (H)	Protects against all but the top 16% of an average threat population
Moderate (M)	Protects against the average threat agent
Low (L)	Only protects against bottom 16% of an average threat population
Very Low (VL)	Only protects against bottom 2% of an average threat population

Table 6.3 Ratings for the values of Control Strength

The question sometimes comes up: "Aren't good hiring practices a control for internal assets?" and "Isn't the lock on the executive's door a control?" Absolutely, they are. But these controls factor into the frequency of contact, as opposed to how effective the controls are at the point of attack.

Derive Vulnerability (Vuln)

Deriving vulnerability is easy once you've established your Tcap and CS. Recall from Section 5.2 that vulnerability is the difference between the force that's likely to be applied, and the asset's ability to resist that force. Using the matrix below, simply find the Tcap along the left side of the matrix, and the CS along the bottom. Where they intersect determines the vulnerability.

Vulnerability

Tcap \ CS	VL	L	M	H	VH
VH	VH	VH	VH	H	M
H	VH	VH	H	M	L
M	VH	H	M	L	VL
L	H	M	L	VL	VL
VL	M	L	VL	VL	VL

Control Strength

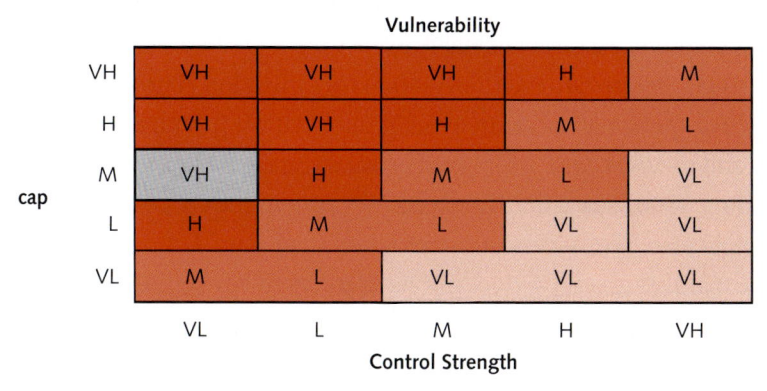

Figure 6.1: Deriving vulnerability

Derive Loss Event Frequency (LEF)

Similar to vulnerability, LEF is derived by intersecting TEF and Vulnerability within a matrix.

Loss Event Frequency

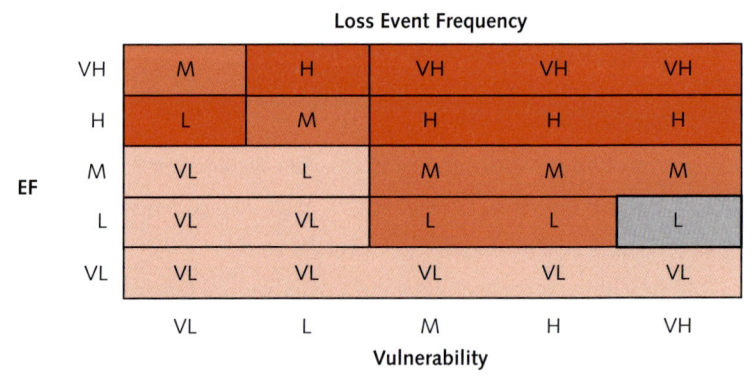

EF \ Vulnerability	VL	L	M	H	VH
VH	M	H	VH	VH	VH
H	L	M	H	H	H
M	VL	L	M	M	M
L	VL	VL	L	L	L
VL	VL	VL	VL	VL	VL

Figure 6.2: Deriving Loss Event Frequency

In our scenario, given a TEF of Low and a Vulnerability of Very High, the LEF is Low. Keep in mind that vulnerability is a percentage, which means that you can never be more than 100% vulnerable. Consequently, LEF will never be greater than TEF.

6.2.3 Stage 3: Evaluate Probable Loss Magnitude (PLM)

Using the previous seven steps, we have determined that the probability of a loss event in our scenario is Low (somewhere between 0.1 and 1 times per year). Now we're faced with analyzing loss if an event does occur.

As mentioned earlier, the username and password credentials inherit the value and liability associated with the resources they provide access to. For an HR executive, we can reasonably expect these credentials to provide access to HR organizational information (organization charts, etc.), as well as employee personal and employment information (performance data, health and medical data, address, SSN, salary, etc.). In some organizations, depending upon where the HR executive exists in the corporate hierarchy, they might also have access to corporate strategy data. For our scenario, we'll assume that this executive does not have access to key sensitive corporate strategies.

Estimate worst-case loss

Within this scenario, three potential threat actions stand out as having significant loss potential, as follows:

- Misuse – employee records typically have information that can be used to execute identity theft, which introduces potential legal and reputation loss.
- Disclosure – employee records often have sensitive personal information related to medical or performance issues, which introduces legal and reputation exposure.
- Deny access (destruction) – employee records are a necessary part of operating any business. Consequently, their destruction can introduce some degree of lost productivity.

In some cases it is necessary to evaluate the loss associated with more than one threat action in order to decide which one has the most significant loss potential. For this exercise, we'll select disclosure as our worst-case threat action.

Our next step is to estimate the worst-case loss magnitude for each loss form.

Threat Actions	Loss Forms					
	Productivity	Response	Replacement	Fine/ Judgments	Comp. Adv.	Reputation
Access						
Misuse						
Disclosure	H	H	–	SV	H	SV
Modification						
Deny Access						

Magnitude	Range Low End	Range High End
Severe (SV)	$10000000	–
High (H)	$1000000	$9999999
Significant (Sg)	$100000	$999999
Moderate (M)	$10000	$99999
Low (L)	$1000	$9999
Very Low (VL)	$0	$999

Figure 6.3: Estimating the worst-case loss

Note that we didn't estimate loss magnitude for Replacement. Any time you're evaluating loss and one or more of the forms has a loss magnitude of Severe (Sv), it is not worthwhile giving much thought to loss forms having a much lower, or no, loss magnitude. In this case, Replacement doesn't apply because the assets aren't being destroyed.

Our estimates are based on the following rationale:
- Productivity – it's conceivable that productivity losses could be High as employee attention is diverted to this event.
- Response – legal expenses associated with inside and outside legal counsel could be High, particularly if class action lawsuits were filed.
- Fines/Judgments – if the disclosed information included details regarding psychological illness or other sensitive health issues, then legal judgments on behalf of affected employees could be Severe, particularly if a large number of employees were affected.

If the information included evidence of criminal activity or incompetence on the part of management, then legal and regulatory fines and sanctions could be Severe.
- Competitive Advantage – if the disclosed information provided evidence of incompetence or criminal activity, competitors could, in theory, leverage that to gain advantage. For the most part, however, we can expect competitors to simply sit back and rake in any disaffected customers (falls under reputation loss).
- Reputation – if the information was sensitive enough, due diligence was seriously absent, legal actions were large enough, and media response was negative and pervasive, then reputation loss associated with customer flight and stock value could be Severe.

Note: Magnitudes will vary based on the size of the organization.

We are not going to document all of our rationale in most risk analyses. Most of the time, we internalize all but the most significant factors. Nonetheless, having a deeper understanding of what these factors are and how they work increases the quality of our analyses.

Note that the rationale above is based on what *could* happen. This highlights the fact that worst-case analyses tend to be based on possibilities rather than probabilities. In order to make this worst-case information meaningful, we need to have some idea of how probable a worst-case outcome is.

A large number of factors affect the likelihood of a worst-case outcome. In this scenario, we selected disclosure as our worst-case threat action, yet we haven't considered the likelihood that a threat agent from this threat community would intentionally disclose the information. Other actions might be far more likely. Accidental disclosure might result, of course, if the threat agent performed identity theft, was caught, and the information was traced back to this organization and this event – a series of "ifs", each with less than 100% probability. Furthermore, even if disclosure occurred, the organization has an opportunity to mitigate loss magnitude through its response. Does it go out of its way to rectify the situation? Does it have an effective public relations capability and a good relationship with the media? Each of these factors reduces the probability of a worst-case outcome.

In most cases it isn't worthwhile spending too much time and effort evaluating the probability of a worst-case outcome. Spend enough time to get a sense for what the key factors are, and roughly where on the continuum worst-case outcome falls between almost certain and almost impossible.

For our scenario, we'll determine that worst-case magnitude is severe (tens of millions of dollars), but with a very low probability of occurring.

Estimate Probable Loss Magnitude (PLM)
The first step in estimating PLM is to determine which threat action is most likely. Remember; actions are driven by motive, and the most common motive for illicit action is financial gain. Given this threat community, the type of asset (personal information), and the available threat actions, it is reasonable to select Misuse as the most likely action; e.g., for identity theft.

Our next step is to estimate the most likely loss magnitude resulting from Misuse for each loss form.

	Loss Forms					
Threat Actions	Productivity	Response	Replacement	Fine/ Judgments	Comp. Adv.	Reputation
Access						
Misuse	M	M	VL	VL	VL	VL
Disclosure						
Modification						
Deny Access						

Magnitude	Range Low End	Range High End
Severe (SV)	$10000000	–
High (H)	$1000000	$9999999
Significant (Sg)	$100000	$999999
Moderate (M)	$10000	$99999
Low (L)	$1000	$9999
Very Low (VL)	$0	$999

Figure 6.4: Estimating Probable Loss Magnitude

Our rationale for these estimates includes:
- The impact to productivity will be Moderate as employees react to the event.
- The cost of responding to the event will include investigation, some amount of time from internal legal counsel, and providing restitution to any affected employees.
- Replacement expenses simply entail the cost of changing the executive's password.
- No legal or regulatory action occurs because the incident isn't taken to court or reported to the regulators.
- No competitive advantage loss occurs due to the relatively inconsequential nature of the event.
- No material reputation damage occurs because it was an internal event, no customers were affected, and the organization had a security program in place that included policies and education.

A few key assumptions also played a role in our estimates, as follows:
- The organization became aware of the incident. It's entirely possible for this kind of event to go undetected. Until detected, there is no material loss to the organization.
- Relatively few employees actually experienced identity theft.

The organization responded effectively to the event.

6.2.4 Stage 4: Derive and articulate risk

Derive and articulate risk

We've already done the hard part, as risk is simply derived from LEF and PLM. The question is whether to articulate risk qualitatively using a matrix like the one below, or articulate risk as LEF, PLM, and worst-case. For this exercise, we'll do both.

Assuming that the matrix below has been "approved" by the leadership of our fictional bank, we can report that risk associated with this threat community is Medium based upon a low LEF (between 0.1 and 1 times per year) and a moderate PLM (between $10K and $100K). Furthermore, we can communicate to our decision-makers that worst-case loss could be severe, but that the probability of a worst-case outcome is very low.

	VL	L	M	H	VH
Severe	H	H	C	C	C
High	M	H	H	C	C
Significant	M	M	H	H	C
Moderate	L	M	M	H	H
Low	L	L	M	M	M
Very Low	L	L	M	M	M

LEF

Key	Risk Level
C	Critical
H	High
M	Moderate
L	Low

Figure 6.5: Derive and articulate risk

In a real analysis, it's likely that we would evaluate and report on more than one threat community.

6.3 Further information

Appendix A provides more detailed discussion of risk taxonomy considerations.

Appendix A Risk taxonomy considerations

Extensive discussion in development of this Risk Taxonomy included considerations that can be grouped into four categories, as follows:
- Concerns regarding complexity of the model
- The availability of data to support statistical analyses
- The iterative nature of risk analyses
- Perspective

Many of these considerations are not so much critical of the FAIR framework, but rather are observations and concerns that apply no matter what method is used to analyze risk.

A.1 Complexity of the model

There is no question that the proposed framework goes into greater detail than most (if any other) risk models. And, if usage of the framework required analyses at the deepest layers of granularity, then it would indeed be impractical for most risk analyses. Fortunately, most analyses can be performed using data and/or estimates at higher levels of abstraction within the model (e.g., measuring Threat Event Frequency rather than attempting to measure Contact Frequency and Probability of Action). This flexibility within the framework allows the user to choose the appropriate level of analysis depth based on their available time, data, as well as the complexity and significance of the scenario being analyzed.

Of course, the fact that the framework includes greater detail provides several key advantages:
- The aforementioned flexibility to go deep when necessary
- A greater understanding of contributing factors to risk
- The ability to better troubleshoot/critique analysis performed at higher layers of abstraction

Another consideration to keep in mind is that risk is inherently complex. If it were not, then we would not need well-defined frameworks and we would not have challenges over analyzing it and communicating about it. Using over-simplified and informal models almost invariably results in unclear and inconsistent assumptions, leading to flawed conclusions, and therefore false recommendations. With that in mind, we recognize that even FAIR's detailed taxonomy isn't a perfect or comprehensive treatment of the problem. There are no perfect taxonomies/models of real-world complexity. It's just that we consider FAIR to be significantly more complete than what we're used to, and the best-analyzed and well-defined there is today.

With regard to communicating complex risk information to business decision-makers (who often want information like this delivered in simple form), the problem isn't inherently with the model but rather with the user. As is the case with any complex problem, we need to be able to articulate results in a way that is useful and digestible to decision-makers. It is also not unusual for management to ask how the results were arrived at. Experience has shown that having a rigorous framework to refer to in the explanation tends to improve credibility and acceptance of the results.

A.2 Availability of data

In risk assessments, good data is especially difficult to acquire for infrequent events. In the absence of such data, how do we arrive at valid frequency estimates?

Good data has been and will continue to be a challenge within our problem space for some time to come. In part, this stems from the absence of a detailed framework that:
- Defines which metrics are needed
- Provides a model for plugging in the data so that meaningful results can be obtained

The FAIR framework has been proven in practice to help solve those two issues. It doesn't, of course, help us with those instances where data isn't available because events are rare. In those cases, regardless of what analysis method is chosen, the estimates aren't going to be as well substantiated by data. On the other hand, the absence of data due to the infrequency of events *is* data – of sorts – and can be used to help guide our estimates. As additional information is acquired over time, it is possible to adjust the initial estimates.

A.3 Iterative risk analyses

Due to the inherent complexity of risk, risk analyses tend to be iterative in nature. In other words, it is absolutely true that initial risk analyses tend to be "sighting shots" that often become more precise as additional analyses are performed. Furthermore, there comes a point of diminishing returns beyond which additional precision is not warranted given the necessary time and expense of deeper/broader analyses.

It is worthy of note that this observation is true of any analysis method, including the FAIR model.

A.4 Perspective

An alternative view held by some is that "exposure" should be the focus of our attention rather than "risk". The argument put forward here is that they consider "risk" to be the inherent worst-case condition, and "exposure" represents the residual risk after controls were applied.

Setting aside the possibility that those who hold this view misinterpret the definition of risk within the FAIR model, both issues are related (sort of a "before" and "after" perspective) and relevant. Fortunately, the FAIR framework provides the means to analyze both conditions by allowing the analyst to derive unmitigated risk as well as mitigated risk levels.

PART 2 THE OPEN GROUP TECHNICAL GUIDE
Requirements for risk assessment methodologies

Chapter 1 Introduction to requirements for risk assessment methodologies 48
Chapter 2 What makes a good risk assessment methodology? 51
Chapter 3 Risk assessment methodology considerations 56
Chapter 4 Assessment elements 60

Chapter 1 Introduction to requirements for risk assessment methodologies

Over time, the information security/risk management profession has developed a variety of methods for assessing risk within an organization. These methods often reflect the conditions and objectives of the organization being assessed (as understood by the assessor), the prevailing practices within the profession at the time, the experience and knowledge level of the assessor(s), as well as any bias or agenda the assessor(s) might bring to the table. Another important factor that has often played a role is the definition of "risk" as used within the methodology.

As a result of these variables, risk assessment results have varied widely in terms of consistency, accuracy, and utility to management. This part seeks to identify and articulate the characteristics that make up effective risk assessment methodologies, thus providing a standard set of guidelines for risk assessment methodologies.

1.1 Business case for risk assessment methodologies

In the overall context of risk management, it is important to appreciate that our business objective in performing risk assessments is to identify and estimate levels of exposure to the likelihood of loss, so that business managers can make informed business decisions on how to manage those risks of loss – either by accepting each risk, or by mitigating it – through investing in appropriate internal protective measures judged sufficient to lower the potential loss to an acceptable level, or by investing in external indemnity. Critical to enabling good business decision-making therefore is to use risk assessment methods which give the most objective, meaningful, consistent results.

With this in mind, a number of challenges exist as a result of the current risk assessment methodology landscape, including:
- Assessment results can't reliably be compared, either between different organizations/scenarios or even amongst assessments performed on a single organization. Consequently, risk posture comparisons and trend analyses within and between industries are difficult if not impossible. Likewise, tracking risk posture improvement within an organization becomes challenging.

- Management and others needing to select and perform a risk assessment may not be able to differentiate more effective methodologies from less effective ones. As a result, their chosen methodology may not provide them with the information they need.

Those developing risk assessment methodologies will continue to introduce variability into the landscape, exacerbating the current condition.

1.2 Scope

In order to provide guidance without unnecessarily limiting assessment methodology evolution or the ability to craft proprietary assessment practices, coverage in this part is limited to describing foundational characteristics that describe effective methodologies. It does not describe a specific methodology.

1.3 Using this Technical Guide

This Guide may be used to help:
- Evaluate whether a given risk assessment methodology meets management needs
- Distinguish between methodologies in order to choose the one that most closely meets management needs
- Evaluate whether a given methodology effectively assesses risk (rather than simply some sub-element of risk; e.g., control conditions)
- As a reference for developing or evolving risk assessment methodologies

1.4 Definition of terms

This Guide takes advantage of the terminology provided in The Open Group Technical Standard: Risk Taxonomy (Part 1 of this book). Borrowing from that part, the following key definitions apply here:
- Risk — The probable frequency and probable magnitude of future loss.
- Threat — Anything that is capable of acting in a manner resulting in harm to an asset and/or organization; for example, acts of God (weather, geological events, etc.), malicious actors, errors, failures.
- Vulnerability — The probability that threat capability exceeds the ability to resist the threat.

- Asset Any data, device, or other component of the environment that supports information-related activities, which can be illicitly accessed, used, disclosed, altered, destroyed, and/or stolen, resulting in loss.

1.5 Key operating assumptions

Before describing requirements, it is important to lay out the key operating assumptions that drive those requirements. Keeping in mind the adage that it's best to "begin with the end in mind", this part will describe assumptions about the fundamental purpose that risk assessments serve (i.e., results). These assumptions about results will then drive assumptions and requirements for the methods used to achieve those results:

- An organization's management team is responsible for seeing that the organization's objectives are met.
- Management has a finite set of resources available in order to meet those objectives.
- There exists a broad spectrum of risk conditions that can interfere in meeting those objectives.
- Management needs accurate and useful information regarding the risk issues it faces and the options it has available so that it can cost-effectively apply its limited resources to the portfolio of risk issues.
- Risk management decisions may, on occasion, have to be defended to key stakeholders (e.g., auditors, regulators, business partners, judges/juries, investors, etc.).
- Risk assessments are intended to provide management with the accurate and useful information needed to make timely, well-informed, effective, and defensible risk management decisions.

Chapter 2 What makes a good risk assessment methodology?

It is important that the information provided by the risk assessment is meaningful to both IT and non-IT management. There is one key component and several key traits that can help a risk assessment methodology provide meaning to an organization.

2.1 Key component: taxonomy

First and foremost, the risk management framework should provide a taxonomy for risk. Taxonomies are used to help those who study a certain body of knowledge to describe and define their problem space. A taxonomy provides a means for categorizing the information around us and helps organize the volumes of information in the field, increase the effectiveness of communication, and develop standardization.

A taxonomy for risk should seek to remove the ambiguity from terms such as threat, vulnerability, and risk (itself having valid but similar definitions to threat and vulnerability).

2.2 Key risk assessment traits

This section describes the traits that are indicative of a good risk assessment methodology. The set of traits provided is by no means complete or comprehensive, but establishes the fundamental concepts that risk assessment methodology development should strive for.

2.2.1 Probabilistic

A study and analysis of risk is a difficult task. Such an analysis involves a discussion of potential states, and it commonly involves using information that contains some level of uncertainty. And so, therefore, an analyst cannot exactly know the risk in past, current, or future state with absolute certainty.

But ultimately a statement concerning risk is a belief statement – a belief statement that is simply the act of describing the issue currently at hand (sometimes referred to as a "state of nature") based on the evidence available at the time. The act of creating a belief statement based on evidence lends itself to using probabilistic methods. Treating risk as a probability problem can add needed rigor, scrutiny, and structure to the risk analysis process and outcome.

A good risk assessment methodology will be organized so as to assist the analyst in creating probabilities for risk and its component factors.

2.2.2 Accurate

A good risk assessment methodology should deliver accurate results. And while it seems self-evident that the results of the risk assessment should be accurate, many risk assessment methodologies focus more on the technical aspects of system weakness instead of the probability of exploitation and resultant impact.

How can we test for accuracy?

The easiest way we can examine a risk statement for accuracy is by comparing past experience to what the assessment says is most probable in frequency and magnitude of loss. For example, if the risk assessment says that the current risk due to exposure of paper information is "high", an organization may be able to compare that result to a past history (i.e., have there been a significant number of past incidents? And if there are occurrences of such incidents, were the costs of those incidents in line with the expected loss amount given in the risk assessment?).

However, quality historical data may be difficult to obtain. In the absence of historical data of acceptable quality, accuracy may be established by:
- Treating risk in a probabilistic manner
- Making sure that variables aren't weighted (unless there is a logical and defensible rationale for doing so)
- Basing the analysis on a risk model that accounts for the reasons why critical aspects of risk exist (e.g., frequency, or the relative capability of the threat, or probable instead of worst-case impact, etc.)

Precision, accuracy, and meaningful results

One of the greatest obstacles for adoption of risk in an organization is the notion that precision is required. Precision in measurement is desirable, but not as necessary as accuracy. Accuracy is best defined for use in risk analysis as "our capability to provide correct information". Precision, however, is defined as "exact, as in performance, execution, or amount". Because risk is a probability problem, it is extremely difficult to be precise in measurement, calculation, and expression. Accuracy may or may not be attainable.

Fortunately for most decisions in information risk management, precise expressions of probable frequency of loss or probable magnitude of loss are not necessary, especially when the risk assessment methodology is capable of consistently delivering accurate results. One of the goals in risk measurement and expression should be to achieve accuracy in the belief statements it creates.

Misrepresentation of precision and creating accuracy
Because achieving high precision in risk assessments is extremely difficult, any assessment that uses falsely precise probability estimates can mislead the decision-maker into believing that there is more rigor in the risk assessment process than actually exists. Accuracy, however, can be provided in risk assessments by using ranges or distributions of estimates and measurements, and communicating the outcome probabilities in terms of ranges or distributions.

2.2.3 Consistent (repeatable)

One significant indicator of a good risk assessment methodology is that it lends itself to repeatable results. That is, if two analysts were given the same information independently and performed a risk assessment, they would arrive at similar conclusions.

This consistency is important for two significant reasons. First, repeatable results validate a degree of rigor and logic within the assessment methodology and model. Second, consistency is critical in creating a defensible, credible belief statement.

2.2.4 Defensible

In order for risk assessment results to be defensible, the results have to be deemed accurate and logical. If the results or measurements of the risk assessment cannot be defended, the recommendation, assessment effort, and presenter all lose credibility.

2.2.5 Logical

One of the most common complaints about risk assessment frameworks is the lack of logic that goes into creating the relationships between the various factors they use to create a risk statement. A good risk assessment methodology will use a model that logically describes how the world works by establishing how the elements of the assessment affect each other and then culminate in that "state of nature" ultimately described as risk. It will not allow for contradictory or haphazard association of risk factors.

Nor will a good risk assessment framework allow for mathematical expression that is nonsensical. For example, many risk assessment frameworks that advocate the use of ordinal scales also advocate the use of arithmetic functions on those values, and as such their results are not logical, consistent, nor defensible.

2.2.6 Risk-focused

The only metrics that really matter are the probable frequency of loss event, and the probable magnitude of loss. As a result, any assessment methodology whose end result cannot be expressed in these terms is not really measuring risk, and is not providing data owners with the information necessary to make a good risk decision. A risk-focused assessment methodology will result in end expressions that are concise and meaningful.

2.2.7 Concise and meaningful

The risk expression must give the right information to the right audience; e.g., executive information must help executives identify their opportunity to mitigate, accept, or transfer risk, and technical information should be provided to enable technical stakeholders to implement selected solution sets. Risk assessment results should be expressed as concisely as possible to lessen the opportunity for confusion. Technical elaborations on controls and attack techniques should be used judiciously.

In order to be meaningful, recommendations from the results of an analyst must also be feasible and actionable in order to allow the data owner to make the best decision given the information at hand.

2.2.8 Feasible

Meaningful outcomes of a risk assessment will also provide feasible options to the decision-maker. Feasible options will be cost-effective, politically viable, and achievable from a technical and execution perspective. Feasible solution sets will also be actionable to give data owners a clear path to the solution under consideration.

2.2.9 Actionable

When confronted with a probability statement around risk, management can mitigate, transfer, or accept/tolerate the issue at hand. Risk assessment results should not only provide management with feasible solution sets, but also include a plan of action (should management decide that action is necessary). Actionable results expression will allow management to properly prioritize their resource allocations.

2.2.10 Prioritized

The results of a risk assessment should help management to be efficient in applying finite resources to the portfolio of business opportunities and risk issues they face. Prioritization may be based on risk, resources required to address the issues, and/or some other criteria provided by management. The bottom line is that prioritization should meet the requirements laid down by management in advance of report generation.

2.2.11 Important note

No amount of risk information, regardless of how accurate or useful, will guarantee good risk decisions on the part of management. Good risk information simply *informs* business managers so they are in the best informed positions to make cost-effective risk management decisions that are based on consistent application of their corporate policy for managing risk.

Chapter 3 Risk assessment methodology considerations

Many risk assessment methodologies tend to focus on providing a step-by-step process for risk assessment without discussing how things should be measured, or at times even what the assessor should be using to create measurement. But even a good risk assessment methodology will provide poor results if some critical aspects of the measurement and calculation process are not considered.

These considerations, described in the following sections, generally boil down to understanding "what" and "how" to measure and calculate. When risk assessments, or risk assessment frameworks, fail it is often because the framework or assessor didn't fully comprehend the implications of what they were measuring and how they were going about measuring those things.

Understanding how the assessment should go about measuring, calculating, and expressing risk is critical to creating a logical, defensible assessment.

3.1 Use of qualitative versus quantitative scales

Current approaches to risk assessment use either qualitative or quantitative means to measure, estimate, and express risk. Ideally, a risk assessment methodology will be useful regardless of which scale is chosen. Note that with quality information available to the assessor, the same risk assessment will produce acceptably similar results when both qualitative and quantitative assessments are performed.

The decision to use one means of expression over another is going to be primarily dependent on two factors:
1. Suitability within the organization
2. Quality of available information

Using qualitative scales requires a description of the boundaries across each level. This can be done using other qualitative words (e.g., "substantial" *versus* "moderate") or quantitative ranges. In the first case, the method is still vulnerable to analyst bias and perception, and mathematical functions can't be applied. In the second case, some math may be feasible depending on how the ranges are structured.

3.1.1 When is using numbers not quantitative?

The use of numbers in an ordinal scale (see section 3.2.2 below) is actually a qualitative approach to risk expression.

If an analyst using a qualitative approach is pressured hard enough, they often reveal (many times to their own surprise) that they are in fact defining their qualitative values using quantitative ranges.

3.2 Measurement scales

When information is being collected for the risk assessment, that information will invariably be ordered in some method of scale. One of the most significant issues with modern risk assessment frameworks is that they do not provide the assessor with an understanding of how to create scale, or the logical implications of their use of measurements in the context of the chosen scale. Data may be arranged in one of the following methods of scale.

3.2.1 Nominal scale

Using a nominal scale, any number is used as a label. For example, in many sports, the number on a uniform gives no indication of performance and is simply used to identify the athlete. Applying mathematical functions to nominal values is nonsensical.

3.2.2 Ordinal scale

In an ordinal scale, quantitative values are assigned to data, but the numbers are only indicative of some relative position of the information. The amount of difference between two points on the scale is undefined, and so using mathematical functions on an ordinal scale is meaningless.

A child arranging crayons in order of color preference is creating ordinal values.

3.2.3 Interval scale

Using an interval scale, the quantitative values describe the position of data sets, but outside of any fixed point that can be called zero (zero can be an arbitrary point, however). Interval variables can express measurement, but multiplication (and division) cannot be performed (directly) on intervals because the creation of any ratio between measurement is meaningless.

Dates in most western calendars are interval values, as would be Celsius temperatures. They are measurements, but we are still unable to perform mathematical function outside of basic addition and subtraction on them (i.e., June 3rd multiplied by June 7th does not equal June 21st).

3.2.4 Ratio scale

In a ratio scale, numbers indicate some amount of difference, using a fixed zero point. Unlike other scales, ratio variables can have statistical functions applied to them because the origin point is not arbitrary.

Examples of ratio values would be Kelvin temperatures, population distribution percentiles, two and three-dimensional space measurements, etc.

3.2.5 Important note

In scales and measurement, only ratio or interval scales can be said to have units of measurement.

3.3 How frequent is 'likely'?

Many approaches to risk assessment attempt to craft a probability expression using a "likelihood" factor. Unfortunately, it is not always evident what likelihood describes and what factors a likelihood expression takes into account. There are two critical flaws in using likelihood:
1. Likelihood usually doesn't describe timeframe (i.e., likely to happen this week, month, year, lifetime, etc.).
2. Likelihood doesn't allow distinctions between events likely to happen once versus many times.

A superior approach is to frame the probability in the context of a timeframe. By introducing the concept of frequency into the probability expression, the risk expression:
- Is framed using an actual measurement (time) allowing for the use of mathematic function
- Becomes more accurate by using time as a factor to refine the probability statement
- Helps simplify the prioritization effort due to clearer communication
- Helps the analyst better identify effective strategies in preventing, detecting, and responding to threat communities

Note: With some audiences, the absence of timeframing in a likelihood expression could call into question whether that expression is simply a discussion of what is possible, rather than a true expression of probability.

3.4 Risk and the data owners

Risk is not a security problem, it is a business problem that surrounds business processes and involves multiple stakeholders. Yet many risk management frameworks don't dive deeply enough into what creates real monetary loss to facilitate the involvement of other subject matter experts in the business. Quality information involves getting subject matter expert estimates and measurements, and many times this will require input from outside information technology. For example, a line of business owner is in the best position to provide estimates surrounding the losses an organization might encounter if a factory is unable to produce product. A marketing department might be the best source of information for monetary amounts that might need to be spent to repair reputation damage.

A good risk assessment effort may require the involvement from marketing, legal, and the data owners. A good risk assessment framework will facilitate the involvement of stakeholders outside of information technology.

Chapter 4 Assessment elements

When executing a risk assessment, the analyst performs two critical functions:
1. The *analysis* of a state of nature (the current observed state of what is being analyzed) using information and evidence to create a state of knowledge (meaning that can be logically arrived at from the evidence in the state of nature)
2. The *synthesis* of wisdom from the state of knowledge

There are five primary elements to an effective risk assessment:
- Identifying risk issues (analysis)
- Evaluating the severity/significance of risk issues (analysis)
- Identifying the root cause of risk issues (synthesis)
- Identifying cost-effective solution options (synthesis)
- Communicating the results to management (synthesis)

4.1 Identifying risk issues

The first element to performing an effective risk assessment is to identify the nature and scope of the assessment. Risk assessments can be performed for isolated business processes or systems, or on an aggregate level. There are several ways in which an analyst can establish evidence for use in risk analysis:
- Interviews and questionnaires
- Testing
- Sampling

4.1.1 Interviews and questionnaires

When developed from a good framework or inventory of controls, assets, business processes, etc., questionnaires can be used as a discovery mechanism for evidence concerning the current state of risk, as well as the organization's ability to manage risk.

Advantages of using interviews and questionnaires

Interviews and questionnaires can help analysts quickly identify areas of concern in an organization's ability to manage risk. The interview and questionnaire process can have less of an impact on organizational resources than more involved means of identifying risk issues such as "red team" or "blue team" testing exercise (and are generally less risky). Interviews and questionnaires are also the most useful way of establishing measurement ranges for use in risk analysis.

Disadvantages of using interviews and questionnaires
The difficulty of developing truly useful questions is widely underestimated. It is no small task to develop questions that protect against bias, encourage consistent and accurate answers, and result in useful measurement.

4.1.2 Testing

Testing can be used in two significant ways in the identification process.

First, testing may be used to uncover evidence of a risk issue. This is most commonly a result of a vulnerability management process such as scanning systems and/or penetration testing. Testing, however, primarily uncovers evidence that equates to symptoms. Testing as a primary discovery method should be followed by interviews and questions developed to help uncover the root cause of the problem and the extent to which the problem exists.

Second, if interviews and/or questionnaires were the primary information gathering process, then testing can be used to help reinforce, or identify discrepancies from, the measurements created by answers to the questionnaire. This use of testing as verification can lead to increased accuracy in the measurement of factors that contribute to risk.

Advantages of using testing
Testing uncovers evidence where the risk management processes may be less than ideal or deviates from the expectations set in policies. Testing can also give very good evidence of an organization's ability to resist a threat of some capability.

Disadvantages of using testing
The data that testing establishes is rarely a direct correlation to the current state of controls, and "passing" a test can lead to a false sense of security. Testing can have negative impacts when performed on an operating environment. It can be more expensive than other review options. Testing is often performed without defining a level of attack sophistication, so testing that is performed with a significant level of attack sophistication can result

in discovering and exploiting a "long tail" issue. Testing can be resource-intensive.

4.1.3 Sampling

Sampling is the act of examining some subset of an overall population in order to extract key characteristics for analysis. Sampling can be useful when:
- Resource requirements to examine the entire population are infeasible.
- The bounds (or frame) of the population is uncertain.

The ability to extract useful information while limiting resource requirements can be a very attractive proposition, but in order to establish a meaningful data set, sampling must be performed well.

In order to sample, the purpose must be well defined. Aspects of purpose definition include:
- The definition of the population should be as specific as possible.
- The unit of sample must be defined.
- The sampling performance should be as unbiased as possible.
- The measurement should be as accurate as possible.

4.1.4 Types of sampling

There are two types of sampling: probability sampling and non-probability sampling. Probability sampling methods that "frame" the data set can greatly assist the organization's ability to organize its data sets. For example, an organization may use stratified sample framing to separate systems or business processes into areas that share characteristics.

4.2 Evaluating the severity/significance of risk issues

The severity of a risk issue is determined through risk analysis. A risk analysis is the process by which the analyst can establish probability statements concerning the frequency and impact of a loss event. These probabilities will be established using information collected by the analyst for the various risk factors.

For example, in order to use the Factor Analysis of Information Risk (FAIR) framework, the analyst will need to collect useful information concerning the frequency of threat events, the capabilities of the threat community in question, the organization's ability to resist the actions of the threat community, and where (and in what form) monetary losses can be expected to affect the organizational budgets.

Once that information is collected, the analyst then can create further (calculated) information concerning the ability of the organization to resist threat actions (i.e., its vulnerability), the probable frequency of loss events, and the probable magnitude of loss events. The combination of these elements is used to establish and communicate the current state of risk for the issue being analyzed.

4.3 Identifying the root cause of risk issues

In order to successfully address risk, an organization must identify the root causes of its risk issues. Root causes generally stem from either a problem in decision-making or execution of decisions that have been made. Root causes with their sources in organizational decision-making exist because of misalignment with management risk tolerances or because management was given inaccurate information regarding risk. Root causes stemming from execution failures exist because of inadequate awareness, capabilities, and/or motivation on the part of those responsible for protecting/managing assets. Identifying root causes is necessary in order for an organization to identify truly successful solution options.

4.4 Identifying cost-effective solution options

Risk assessments should present decision-makers with options for risk treatment (where reasonable options exist). This requires that analysts present decision-makers with a statement concerning the current state of risk, and either:

- Solutions that will bring the level of risk to an established desired level
- Solutions that will reduce the level of risk to various degrees of magnitude

In either case, the analyst should expect to perform several desired state analyses to allow for more than one solution option for decision-makers. Solutions should consider:

- Resources required to achieve desired or future state
- Comparison of proposed future state(s) with the current state
- Resources required to maintain their future state(s)

If possible, a "side by side" comparison of multiple solutions relative to the current state is desirable. Including the resources required for each solution allows for a cost/benefit comparison.

4.5 Communicating the results to management

4.5.1 What to communicate
Results should communicate:
- The current risk
- Future desired state (if available)
- Root cause of variance between the current state and the desired state
- Various options (and their resource requirements) that will achieve and maintain the desired state

Current and desired states of risk should be expressed using two key measurements:
- The probable frequency with which loss events may occur
- The probable magnitude of loss events

A worst-case loss magnitude may also be expressed to communicate the upper bounds of loss. Various risk reduction statistics can be created by comparing the investment needed and the benefits in either expected frequency or loss magnitude.

4.5.2 How to communicate
The language of the business manager, regulator, legislator, policy-maker, and boardroom is well known to be markedly different to that used by IT technologists. Nowhere is this language gap more pronounced than when talking about "risk" and how to manage it.

This is the prime reason why a rigorous risk taxonomy is needed – to define specific meanings to the key words that all use when talking about risk, so that all can refer to this taxonomy and therefore be sure they mean the same thing.

An example of this language gap is that the business manager talks about "impact" of loss, not in terms of how many servers or operational IT systems will cease to provide normal service, but rather what will be the impact of losing normal service on the business's ability to continue to trade normally and, if there is an impact, what is that when measured in terms of $-value.

The key lesson here is that even the best risk assessment is only of high value to its consumer – the business risk decision-makers – when it is presented in terms which the decision-makers understand and which therefore enable them to make the right decisions to manage the organization's risk profile in line with their risk management policy and the applicable regulatory regime to which they wish to conform.

Many good risk assessments – like many good proposals for investment in information security – have failed to be accepted because one or both parties have not taken sufficient note of how to communicate effectively the key issues on cost of investment, exposure to risks, and return on investment (benefits).

PART 3 THE OPEN GROUP TECHNICAL GUIDE

FAIR–ISO/IEC 27005 Cookbook

Chapter 1 Introduction to the FAIR-ISO/IEC 27005 Cookbook 68
Chapter 2 How to manage risk 70
Chapter 3 What information is necessary for risk analysis 80
Chapter 4 How to use FAIR in your ISMS 89
Appendix A Risk Management Program Worksheet 104

Chapter 1 Introduction to the FAIR–ISO/IEC 27005 Cookbook

1.1 Purpose

The purpose of this Cookbook is to help the security practitioner responsible for their organization's risk estimation function to use The Open Group Risk Management Framework in an ISO/IEC 27005 structured process. This guide discusses the different purposes of the two standards, how to reconcile the two with regard to terminology and process, and how to combine the best elements of both to produce a consistent, repeatable risk management proce

1.2 Scope

This guide does not fully discuss the role of risk management in the context of the security executive's portfolio, the communication of risk, nor the use of metrics in risk estimation or risk management. Rather, it is solely focused on risk management and risk estimation, and how the practitioner can combine FAIR (Factor Analysis for Information Risk) and ISO/IEC 27005 into a robust business process. The examples and "cookbook" approach are designed to give the risk analyst a pragmatic and repeatable process applicable to most of their daily tasks.

1.3 Intended audience

Although this guide addresses ISO/IEC 27005, it is not written in a style and discipline that is consistent with an ISO publication. Instead, it is written in the style of its companion Open Group Risk Management parts of this book:
- Risk Taxonomy Technical Standard (Part 1 of this book)
- Requirements for Risk Management Methodologies Technical Guide (Part 2 of this book)

This is because, like its companion parts, its primary target audience is people who actually "do" risk management rather than write ISO standards.

In this regard, some consideration has been given to the notion that anyone interested in presenting this Cookbook using the ISO style and discipline could re-write it so as to position it as an SC27 TR, and thereby perhaps make it more attuned to the expectations of the ISO standards community and its worldwide audience.

1.4 Operating assumptions

It is assumed that:
- The reader is familiar with ISO/IEC 27001 and ISO/IEC 27002.
- The reader is thoroughly familiar with ISO/IEC 27005, and is experienced in using it.
- The reader knows the FAIR risk management approach, as defined in the referenced Open Group Risk Taxonomy Technical Standard, and is familiar with using it.

Clearly the reader with good understanding of risk management and its role in an information security program will be at a considerable advantage. In this respect, the referenced Open Group Requirements for Risk Assessment Methodologies Technical Guide is a recommended reference.

1.5 Using this Cookbook

One of the most significant issues with the current state of information risk management is lack of established nomenclature. Terms such as "threat", "impact", and even "risk" can carry different perspectives and meanings. The first thing the reader may find best to do is review Table 2.2 in Section 2.3 to reconcile terms into a common taxonomy and ontology. Once the reader has digested that information, it may then be advisable to quickly review ISO/IEC 27005 §5 before returning to Chapter 2, though this step is not "required". After reading and following the examples given, the reader is encouraged to attempt risk analysis for themselves using the example as a guideline and Appendix A at the end of part 3 as a template.

In the context of security portfolio management, this document may be applicable to the following enterprise functions:
- Project management
- Resource prioritization
- Security architecture development
- Compliance solution development
- Control solution development

Chapter 2 How to manage risk

2.1 Information Security Management System (ISMS) overview

The reader should already understand that the ISO Information Security Management System (ISMS) is intended to be an organization's strategic plan for information security. This section provides a brief overview of the relevant ISO documents. The relationship of the concepts is shown in Figure 2.1.

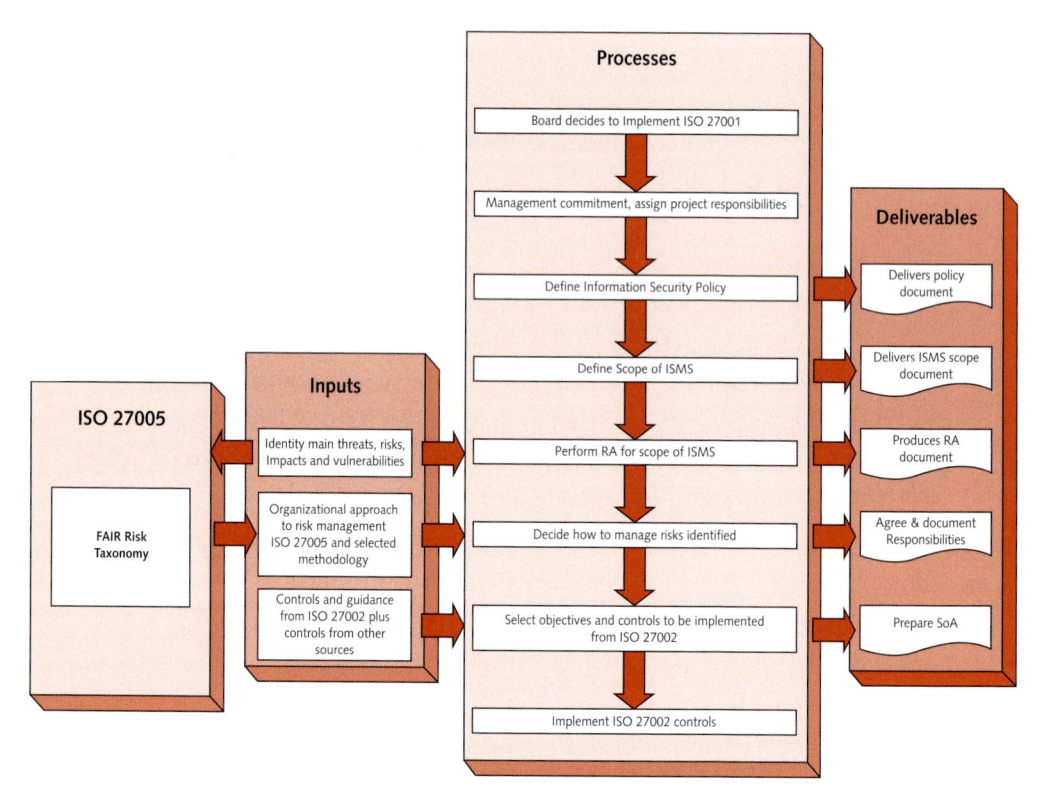

Figure 2.1: Use of ISO/IEC 27005 and FAIR in ISO/IEC 27001 ISMS development processes

ISO provides several documents that offer guidance in developing the ISMS. Those relevant to management of risk are:
- ISO/IEC 27001:2005: Information Technology – Security Techniques – Information Security Management System – Requirements (ISMS):
  - Describes a model for establishing, implementing, operating, monitoring, reviewing, maintaining, and improving an ISMS
  - Used to assess conformance by interested internal and external parties

- Applies to all types of organizations (e.g., commercial enterprises, government agencies, non-profit organizations)
- Ensures selection of adequate and proportionate security controls that protect information assets and give confidence to interested parties
- Specifies requirements for the implementation of security controls customized to the needs of individual organizations or departments
• ISO/IEC 27002:2005: Information Technology – Security Techniques – Code of Practice for Information Security Management (Controls):
  - Provides 12 domains of information security
  - Defines security controls that may be selected within each domain
  - Provides implementation guidance in each area
• ISO/IEC 27005:2008: Information Technology – Security Techniques – Information Security Risk Management:
  - Provides a general approach to risk management
  - Is the primary focus of this document

Since the ISMS is a strategic plan for information security, its development is influenced by the needs and objectives, security requirements, processes, and the size and structure of the organization. Each company's ISMS (and the organization's security environment) is expected to change over time; consequently, ISO's implementation of ISMS uses the "Plan-Do-Check-Act" (PDCA) model. See ISO/IEC 27001 §0.2 for the PDCA model as applied to the ISMS.

Stages of the PDCA model are as follows:
• Plan (establish the ISMS): Establish ISMS policy, objectives, processes, and procedures relevant to managing risk and improving information security to deliver results in accordance with an organization's overall policies and objectives.
• Do (implement and operate the ISMS): Implement and operate the ISMS policy, controls, processes, and procedures.
• Check (monitor and review the ISMS): Assess and, where applicable, measure process performance against ISMS policy, objectives, and practical experience and report the results to management for review.
• Act (maintain and improve the ISMS): Take corrective and preventive actions, based on the results of the internal ISMS audit and management review or other relevant information, to achieve continual improvement of the ISMS.

An ISMS implementation should be scaled in accordance with the organization's needs – a simple situation requires a simple ISMS solution. For an organization to claim conformance to ISO/IEC 27001, none of the requirements specified in Clauses 4, 5, 6, 7, and 8 may be excluded. Any exclusion of controls found to be necessary to satisfy the risk acceptance criteria needs to be justified and evidence needs to be provided that the associated risks have been accepted by the accountable persons. Where any controls are excluded, claims of conformance to ISO/IEC 27001 are not acceptable unless such exclusions do not affect the organization's ability, and/or responsibility, to provide information security that meets the security requirements determined by risk assessment and applicable legal or regulatory requirements.

2.2 How FAIR plugs into the ISMS

ISO/IEC 27001 describes a general process for the ISMS, and in that context ISO/IEC 27005 defines the approach to managing risk. FAIR provides a methodology for analyzing risk. This section describes how the FAIR methodology can be used to analyze risk in the context of ISO/IEC 27005 and the ISMS. Step-by-step details based on these concepts are presented in ISO/IEC 27005 §5.

ISO/IEC 27001 §4.2.1 provides the foundation for the risk management portion of the ISMS:

- Define the risk assessment approach of the organization
- Identify the risks
- Analyze and evaluate the risks
- Identify and evaluate options for the treatment of risks
- Select control objectives and controls for the treatment of risks
- Obtain management approval of the proposed residual risks

This generally outlines the process for managing risk at a very high level.

ISO/IEC 27002 provides the taxonomy of information security controls. Figure 2.2 illustrates how the FAIR framework complements the ISO/IEC 27002 framework. ISO/IEC 27002 §4.0 discusses risk management and treatment as a domain in the ISMS.

ISO/IEC 27005 specifies in more detail the management of risk without providing specifics or identifying a methodology for determining risk level. FAIR provides a methodology to achieve the steps shown above, specifically "identify the risks" and "analyze and evaluate the risks".

Risk Assessment and Treatment
Identify, quantify, and prioritize risks against criteria for risk acceptance and objectives relevant to the organization.
(ISO 27002 4.0)

ISO 27005

FAIR Risk Taxonomy

Security Policy
Provide management, direction, and support for information security in accordance with business requirements and relevant laws and regulations.
(ISO 27002 5.0)

Organization of Information Security
Manage information security within the organization, maintain the security of the organization's information and information assets that are accessed, processed, communicated to, or managed by external parties.
(ISO 27002 6.0)

Asset Management
Achieve and maintain appropriate protection of organizational assets and ensure that information receives an appropriate level of protection.
(ISO 27002 7.0)

Human Resource Security
Ensure that employees, contractors and third party users understand their responsibilities, and to reduce the risk of theft, fraud or misuse of facilities before, during and after employment.
(ISO 27002 8.0)

Physical and Environmental Security
Prevent unauthorized physical access, loss, damage, theft, compromise and interference to the organization's premises, activities and information.
(ISO 27002 9.0)

Communications and Operations Management
Ensure the correct and secure operation of information assets, implement and maintain the appropriate level of information security and service delivery in line with third party service delivery agreements, minimize the risk of system failures, protect the integrity of software and information, maintain the integrity and availability of information assets, prevent unauthorized disclosure, modification, removal or destruction of assets, maintain the security of information and software exchanged within an organization and with any external entity, and detect unauthorized activities.
(ISO 27002 10.0)

Assess Control
Control access to information assets and prevent unauthorized access.
(ISO 27002 11.0)

Information Systems Acquisition, Development and Maintenance
Ensure that security is an integral part of information systems. Prevent errors, loss, unauthorized modification or misuse of information, and protect the confidentiality, authenticity or integrity of information.
(ISO 27002 12.0)

Information Security Incident Management
Ensure information security events and weaknesses associated with information systems are communicated in a manner allowing timely corrective action to be taken and ensure a consistent and effective approach is applied to the management of information security incidents.
(ISO 27002 13.0)

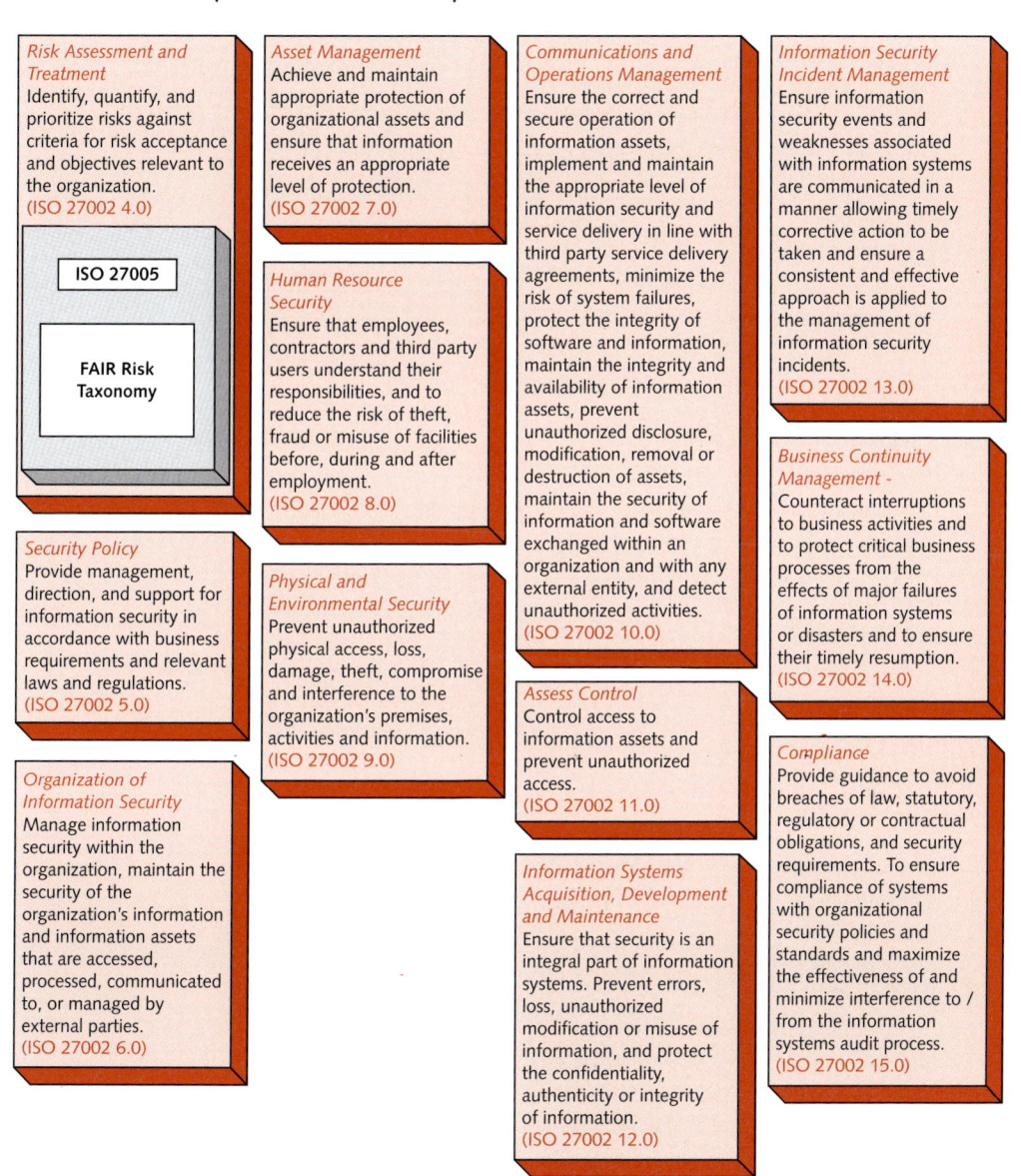

Business Continuity Management -
Counteract interruptions to business activities and to protect critical business processes from the effects of major failures of information systems or disasters and to ensure their timely resumption.
(ISO 27002 14.0)

Compliance
Provide guidance to avoid breaches of law, statutory, regulatory or contractual obligations, and security requirements. To ensure compliance of systems with organizational security policies and standards and maximize the effectiveness of and minimize interference to / from the information systems audit process.
(ISO 27002 15.0)

Figure 2.2: FAIR integrated into ISO/IEC 27002 ISMS controls framework

Table 2.1 shows how the FAIR risk analysis steps relate to the process outlined in ISO/IEC 27005.

7.0	Context Establishment	
7.1	General Considerations	
7.2	Basic Criteria	
7.3	Scope and Boundaries	
7.4	Organization of Information Security Risk Management	
8.0	Information Security Risk Assessment	
8.1	General Description of Information Security Risk Assessment	
8.2	Risk Analysis	Risk Analysis using FAIR
8.2.1	Risk Identification	Stage 1:
8.2.1.1	Introduction to risk identification	Identify scenario components
8.2.1.2	Identification of assets	Identify the asset at risk
8.2.1.3	Identification of threats	Identify the threat community
8.2.1.4	Identification of existing controls	Stage 2:
8.2.1.5	Identification of vulnerabilities	Evaluate Loss Event Frequency (LEF)
8.2.1.6	Identification of consequences	Estimate probable Threat Event Frequency
8.2.2	Risk estimation	(TEF)
8.2.2.1	Risk estimation methodologies	Estimate Threat Capability (TCap)
8.2.2.2	Assessment of consequences	Estimate Control Strength (CS)
8.2.2.3	Assessment of incident likelihood	Derive Vulnerability (Vuln)
8.2.2.4	Level of risk estimation	Derive Loss Event Frequency (LEF)
8.3	Risk Evaluation	Stage 3:
		Evaluate Probable Loss Magnitude (PLM)
		Estimate worst-case loss
		Estimate Probable Loss Magnitude (PLM)
		Stage 4:
		Derive and articulate risk
9.0	Information Security Risk Treatment	
9.1	General Description of Risk Treatment	
9.2	Risk Reduction	
9.3	Risk Retention	
9.4	Risk Avoidance	
9.5	Risk Transfer	
10.0	Information Security Risk Acceptance	
11.0	Information Security Risk Communication	
12.0	Information Security Risk Monitoring and Review	
12.1	Monitoring and Review of Risk Factors	
12.2	Risk Management Monitoring, Reviewing, and Improving	

Table 2.1: FAIR's place within ISO/IEC 27005

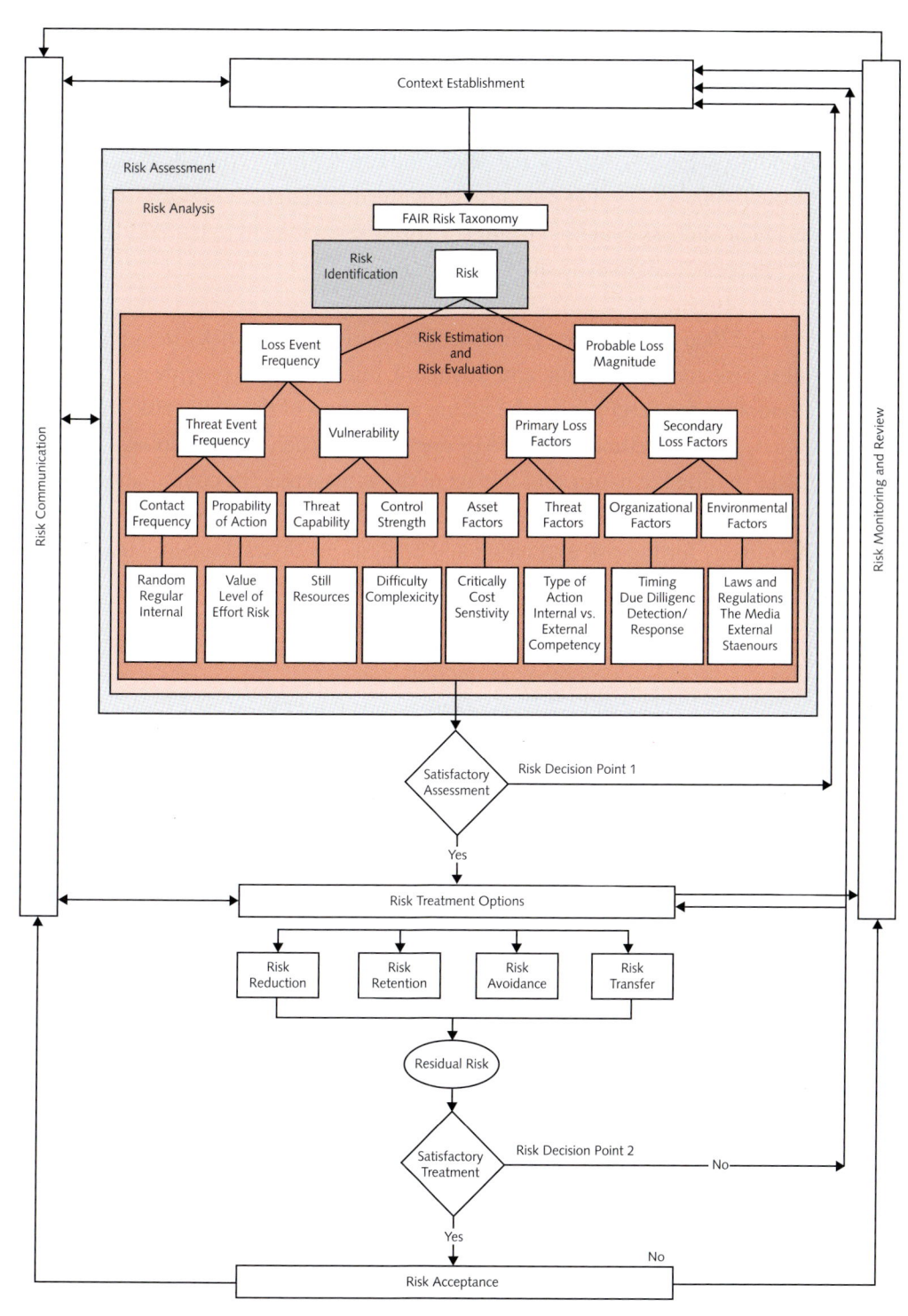

Figure 2.3: ISO/IEC 27005 – FAIR integration model

While ISO/IEC 27001 outlines the process for managing risk at a very high level, by defining the ISMS, ISO/IEC 27005 specifies in more detail the management of risk, although without providing specifics or identifying a methodology for determining risk level. You can see how FAIR fills the gap in ISO/IEC 27005 §8.2 and §8.3 by providing the detailed methodology for risk assessment and risk evaluation, and is a strong complement to the ISO/IEC 27005 process in support of the ISMS.

ISO/IEC 27005 does provide guidelines for development of risk assessment context, risk communication, and treatment, but it does not provide a methodology for determining the nature and impact of the actual risk (risk assessment methodology). FAIR does provide such a methodology for determining the nature and impact of the actual risk. The combination of ISO/IEC 27005 and FAIR can therefore serve as the framework and methodology for the risk evaluation and analysis processes domain. Figure 2.3 (page 75) illustrates the integration of FAIR in the ISO/IEC 27005 framework.

2.3 Major differences in approach

There are numerous differences between ISO/IEC 27005 and FAIR. However, the standards complement each other in many ways. ISO/IEC 27005 provides a framework for a risk management program. It includes concepts such as risk management program development, risk management communication, monitoring, and treatment of risks. FAIR provides an actual methodology for evaluating the probabilities and impacts of actual risks. In other words, FAIR provides the actual methods to meet the needs of ISO/IEC 27005 §8.2 (Risk Analysis) and §8.3 (Risk Evaluation). This can be seen graphically in Figure 2.2 above.

Other differences exist in such items as specific definitions. The following definition differences are dominant (Table 2.2 - page 77).

Term	FAIR Definition	ISO Definition	Specific ISO Reference	Differences
Asset	Any data, device, or other component of the environment that supports information-related activities, which can be illicitly accessed, used, disclosed, altered, destroyed, and/or stolen, resulting in loss.	Anything that has value to the organization.	ISO/IEC 27001 ISO/IEC 27002	ISO provides a simpler, but somewhat vague definition of asset. The FAIR definition looks at assets from the perspective of information security and the principles of confidentiality, integrity, and availability.
Risk	The probable frequency and probable magnitude of future loss.	Combination of the probability of an event and its consequence.	ISO/IEC 27002	These two definitions are nearly identical. The concepts of magnitude and consequence are synonymous. The ISO use of probability can be interpreted as likelihood, while FAIR deliberately uses frequency.
Threat	Anything that is capable of acting in a manner resulting in harm to an asset and/or organization; for example, acts of God (weather, geological events, etc.), malicious actors, errors, failures.	A potential cause of an unwanted incident, which may result in harm to a system or organization.	ISO/IEC 27002	These two definitions are nearly identical.
Vulne-rability	The probability that an asset will be unable to resist actions of a threat agent.	A weakness of an asset or group of assets that can be exploited by one or more threats.	ISO/IEC 27002	ISO focuses on the existence of a weakness whereas FAIR focuses on the asset's ability to resist the actions of a threat agent.

Table 2.2: Differences in ISO/IEC 27005 and FAIR definitions

2.4 Recommended approach

The first step in any risk analysis is to identify the question(s) to be answered. An organization that wants to identify and prioritize security technology investments needs to understand which controls are most important to reduce risk; that is, which controls have both the most influence on risk and are in greater need of improvement. The ISMS defines the management system for establishing a context for risk, and for managing risk decisions. ISO/IEC 27002 provides a taxonomy of security controls, complete with guidelines for evaluating control effectiveness. ISO/IEC 27005 provides the framework for risk management and FAIR provides the methodology for evaluating and quantifying risk. In the following sections we will see how the integration of ISO/IEC 27005 and FAIR provides a method for calculating risk so that these questions can be answered for business owners.

2.5 Points to consider

2.5.1 Concerns about the complexity of the model

The incorporation of FAIR and ISO/IEC 27005 makes a more complex model than either standard on its own. ISO's high-level approach to risk management (determining the context, developing treatment and communications plans), while essential to risk management, adds to the tasks of FAIR.

The FAIR framework goes into greater detail than most risk models. This level of detail provides some advantages:
- Flexibility to go deep when necessary
- Better understanding of factors contributing to risk
- Ability to better troubleshoot analysis performed at higher layers of abstraction

However, if usage of FAIR required analyses at the deepest layers of granularity it would be impractical for risk analysis. Fortunately, FAIR risk assessment can be performed using data/estimates at higher levels of abstraction within the model (for example, measuring Threat Event Frequency (TEF) rather than attempting to measure contact frequency and probability of action). Flexibility within the framework enables the user to choose the appropriate level of analysis, based on the time, data, complexity, and significance of the scenario.

Another consideration relating to complexity is that risk by its very nature is inherently complicated. Over-simplified models lead to false conclusions and recommendations. FAIR's detailed taxonomy may not be a perfect treatment of the problem, but FAIR is considered to be the most complete, best analyzed, and defined methodology/taxonomy available.

Communicating complex risk information to decision-makers presents a problem with any model. As with any complex problem, it is important to articulate results in ways that can be processed most easily and so are most useful to decision-makers. Having a rigorous framework and explaining how the results were arrived at improves credibility and acceptance of the results. Developing a communication plan as prescribed in ISO/IEC 27005 provides guidance to ensure the appropriate information is dispersed to all identified stakeholders.

2.5.2 Availability of data to support statistical analysis

In risk assessment, quality data is difficult to acquire. In the absence of such data, it is hard to achieve valid frequency estimates. This challenge partially originates from the absence of a detailed framework that:

- Defines which metrics are needed
- Provides a model for incorporating the data so that meaningful results can be obtained

2.5.3 The iterative nature of risk analyses

Due to the inherent complexity of risk, analyses tend to be iterative in nature. Developing a treatment plan can introduce other risks that must be evaluated. With each iteration the results become more precise, but there comes a point of diminishing returns beyond which additional precision and evaluation is not warranted, given the time and expense that would be required for further analyses.

Chapter 3 What information is necessary for risk analysis?

3.1 Introduction to the landscape of risk

In general, any risk management/analysis/estimation exercise is an attempt to reconcile the relationships between four dependent sources of information – threat, loss (impact), controls, and assets – into a descriptive point of reference called "risk". Each risk management standard or methodology treats these information "landscapes" in a somewhat subtly different manner from others. For the purposes of helping analysts augment ISO/IEC 27005 processes with a FAIR-based risk estimation, we will begin by comparing the approaches of each standard for each landscape, and discussing in general terms what sort of prior information may contribute to providing context for the factors needed in a FAIR estimation.

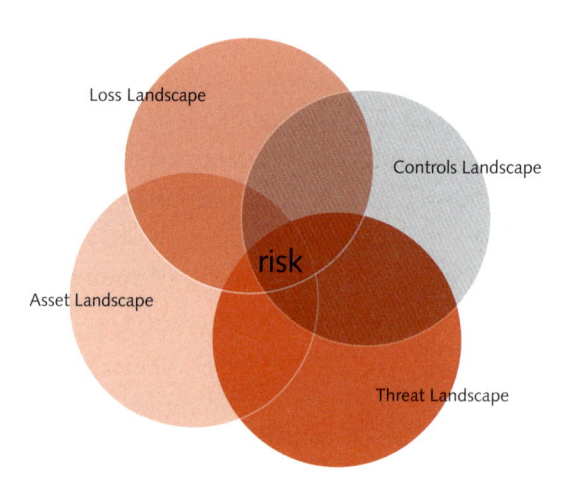

Figure 3.1: Risk landscapes

3.2 Asset landscape

The asset landscape represents information about what is to be protected. To perform a FAIR analysis, the analyst needs to understand the nature of the asset in question and how it relates to each of the other landscapes.

As the asset intersects with the loss or impact landscape, the analyst should understand information including: the business process(es) the asset contributes to, the cost to replace the asset, the architecture of the asset (hardware, software, nature of services accessible, etc.), and the resources necessary to respond to an incident (geographic location in relation to the Incident Response Team, for example).

In considering the threat landscape, the analyst may find it useful to pre-suppose the applicable threat community. In doing so, information about the asset's value to the threat can be considered, as well as the relative frequency and nature of threat contact with the asset in question.

Finally, the analyst should seek to understand aspects of the asset that will contribute to the ability to resist the actions of a threat agent (for example, the architecture of some assets may be more or less prone to vulnerability than others). It may seem to be a semantic distinction, but information regarding the nature of the asset and the organization's ability to manage and maintain the asset contribute to our understanding of the controls landscape.

Other information is useful in generating a generalized "context" as per ISO/IEC 27005, such as the list given on page nine of that document (repeated here for convenience):
- The organization's strategic business objectives, strategies, and policies
- Business processes
- The organization's functions and structure
- Legal, regulatory, and contractual requirements applicable to the organization
- The organization's information security policy
- The organization's overall approach to risk management
- Information assets
- Locations of the organization and their geographical characteristics
- Constraints affecting the organization
- Expectation of stakeholders
- Socio-cultural environment
- Interfaces (i.e., information exchange with the environment)

3.2.1 ISO definition and goal

ISO/IEC 27005 defines an asset as "anything that has value to the organization and which therefore requires protection". The asset identification described in ISO/IEC 27005 §8.2.1.2 suggests that asset identification should be performed at a suitable level for the risk assessment, and that the owner should be identified for each asset. The output of ISO/IEC 27005 §8.2.1.2 is a list of the assets to be risk managed and a list of business processes related to assets and their relevance.

3.2.2 Major differences in asset landscape treatment
The identification of assets for analysis and creation of an asset catalog that includes asset owners and the business processes assets support is useful for analysis using both standards.

3.3 Threat landscape
The threat landscape consists of the information we need to understand about what may act against our asset.

3.3.1 ISO definition and goal
A threat has the potential to harm assets such as information, processes and systems, and therefore, organizations. Threats may be of natural or human origin, and could be accidental or deliberate.

The output is a list of threats with the identification of threat type and source.

3.3.2 Major differences in threat landscape treatment
The most significant differences in threat landscape treatment between The Open Group probabilistic approach and the ISO/IEC 27005 process are:
- The structure of classification
- The consideration of threat actions
- The development of metrics for the threat landscape

3.3.3 Structure of classification
ISO/IEC 27005 treats the concept of a threat as either a cause or effect ,which can be confusing, and leads to significantly more work than is needed to define the relevant aspects of the threat landscape. The Open Group approach breaks threats down by category (human/natural/malware) and then by characteristics (physical and trust relationships to the controls and assets).

An analyst can use The Open Group framework's more rational, descriptive structure in their analysis. This would mean identifying the most probable threat for consideration from one of the following categories (Table 3.1).

Human		Malware	Force Majeure
Internal	**External**	**Malware**	**Force Majeure**
Privileged	Technical Professional	Any self-propagating	Various
Non-Privileged	Technical Amateur		
	Non-Technical Professional		
	Non-Technical Amateur		

Table 3.1 The Open Group's threat classification structure

3.3.4 Consideration of threat actions

The Open Group framework does not specifically address threat actions. An analyst can use the ISO/IEC 27005 list to describe the action that the threat source is most likely to take. The action consideration would then help the analyst to establish metric ranges for the threat landscape.

In our example, given our asset "A" we might ascribe threat action "SQL injection" to the threat community "External Technical Professional". Other external threat frameworks (for example, WASC for web-based attacks) can also be used to describe threat actions within the context of threat modeling for this landscape.

3.3.5 The development of metrics for the threat landscape

To create a probabilistic approach to risk estimation, The Open Group framework requires estimated ranges for two specific metrics:
1. The expected frequency of "threat events"
2. The ability of the threat to apply force against the asset and subsequent controls, or "threat capability"

In developing these threat metrics, the threat classification and probable threat actions should drive the analyst's quest for evidence and subsequent measurements.

In our example, an analyst might seek frequency numbers for SQL injection attempts against asset "A" or significantly similar assets, and then ascribe a range for threat capability based on the strength/complexity of that attack type when compared to other attacks that asset may face.

Once the metrics for the threat landscape are gathered, the next step in risk analysis would be to review the controls landscape, as the ability to resist controls is relative to threat capability (which FAIR defines as the level of force we might expect a threat agent to apply against an asset).

3.4 Controls landscape

3.4.1 ISO definition and goal

ISO/IEC 27005 §8.2.1.4 discusses what is useful for the identification of existing or planned controls for consideration in risk analysis. The input for ISO/IEC 27005 §8.2.1.4 is control documentation and potential risk treatment plans, and the output is a list of all existing and planned controls, their implementation, and usage status.

3.4.2 Major differences in controls landscape treatment

The controls landscape in ISO/IEC 27005 is better defined as what is governed in ISO/IEC 27001. Controls in ISO/IEC 27005 are estimated in "effectiveness" based on their ability to reduce the likelihood and/or ease of vulnerability exploit, and/or the impact of an incident. We might say that in ISO/IEC 27005 controls are judged relative to the exploit (ignoring for a moment a control that reduces impact).

Controls in FAIR are defined as those things that will contribute to an ability to resist a threat community. Control strength is an estimation of the ability to resist the force applied by some percentage of the general threat agent population. We might say that in FAIR an ability to resist is judged relative to the threat population.

3.4.3 Development of metrics for the controls landscape

The primary metric for use in FAIR analysis is control strength. Control strength should be measurement of the ability to resist the force applied by some percentage of the general threat agent population. Information in ISO/IEC 27005 §8.2.1.4 (implementation and usage information) suggests that analysts should gather "control effectiveness" ratings for various controls that are useful in establishing control strength estimates.

3.5 Loss (impact) landscape

3.5.1 ISO definition and goal
ISO/IEC 27005 defines impact as an adverse change to the level of business objectives achieved. ISO/IEC 27005 §8.2.1.6 discusses the identification of consequences that losses of confidentiality, integrity, and availability may have on the assets. A consequence can be loss of effectiveness, adverse operating conditions, loss of business, reputation, damage, etc.

3.5.2 Major differences in loss (impact) landscape treatment
Both approaches share the common challenge of attempting to estimate the value of a loss event.

The loss (impact) landscape in ISO/IEC 27005 uses the technique of incident scenarios (also called security failures in ISO/IEC 27001). Impacts in ISO/IEC 27005 are identified by estimating the damage or consequences to the organization that could be caused by an incident scenario. So ISO produces a list of possible impacts presented as discrete values, sometimes expressed as monetary values.

FAIR focuses on identifying the factors that drive loss magnitude when events occur. An asset's loss potential stems from the value it represents and/or the liability it introduces to an organization. So, FAIR presents loss as a mathematical model of a range of likely monetary values.

3.5.3 Structure of classification
Forms of loss come from two sources. First, there are losses that are primarily (or directly) incurred due to the actions of the threat agent – a lack of productivity, destruction of assets, the cost of incident response. Second, there are losses that an organization encounters when another party acts because of the primary losses – losses that occur due to regulatory fines, class action lawsuits, losses in revenue due to customer churn, etc. Both FAIR and ISO/IEC 27005 classify loss forms in a similar manner, aiding the development of metrics for the loss or impact landscape.

3.5.4 Development of metrics for the loss (impact) landscape

Annex B of ISO/IEC 27005 guides readers to develop loss assessments based on "direct" and "indirect" operational impacts. Similarly, FAIR breaks down loss forms into primary and secondary loss categories. Table 3.2 compares these categories:

FAIR – Primary Losses	ISO/IEC 27005 Direct Operational Impacts
Productivity: The reduction in an organization's ability to generate its primary value proposition (e.g., income, goods, services, etc.).	The financial replacement value of lost (part of) asset.
Response: Expenses associated with managing a loss event (e.g., internal or external person-hours, logistical expenses, etc.).	The cost of acquisition, configuration, and installation of the new asset or back-up.
Replacement: The intrinsic value of an asset. Typically represented as the capital expense associated with replacing lost or damaged assets (e.g., rebuilding a facility, purchasing a replacement laptop, etc.).	The cost of suspended operations due to the incident until the service provided by the asset(s) is restored.
	Impact results in an information security breach.
FAIR – Secondary Losses	**ISO/IEC 27005 Indirect Operational Impacts**
Competitive Advantage – Losses associated with diminished competitive advantage. CA loss is specifically associated with assets that provide competitive differentiation between the organization and its competition. Examples include trade secrets, merger and acquisition plans, etc.	Opportunity cost (financial resources needed to replace or repair an asset would have been used elsewhere).
Fines/Judgments – Legal or regulatory actions levied against an organization. Note that this includes bail for any organization members who are arrested.	The cost of interrupted operations.
Reputation – Losses associated with an external perception that an organization's value proposition is reduced or leadership is incompetent, criminal, or unethical.	Potential misuse of information obtained through a security breach.
	Violation of statutory or regulatory obligations.
	Violation of ethical codes of conduct.

Table 3.2: Comparison of loss categories

3.5.5 Probability of indirect operational impacts

In FAIR analysis, the probability of a primary loss event and the losses we can attribute to that event actually drive the probability of a secondary loss event.

An organization has the opportunity to implement controls that will resist "threats" from identifiable sources of these secondary losses. For example, a primary incident concerning regulated information carries some probability of a second incident where government regulators are a new "threat source". Past audits and other evidence of diligence may serve to help the organization resist (or limit) the force the regulators might apply (their fines).

So, in using a FAIR approach to ISO/IEC 27005 loss estimation would be:
- Identify direct operational impacts
- Identify the source of secondary operational impacts
- Perform subsequent analysis (as warranted) to determine the likelihood and impact of secondary operational impacts

3.6 Vulnerability landscape

3.6.1 ISO definition and goal
ISO/IEC 27005 §8.2.1.5 describes a need to identify vulnerabilities that can be exploited by threats to cause harm to assets. The outcome of §8.2.1.5 is a list of system or process weaknesses.

3.6.2 Major differences in vulnerability landscape treatment
There is no "vulnerability landscape" in Figure 3.1; rather the concept of "vulnerable" describes the information that is represented by where the threat, controls, and asset landscapes intersect. This is because, in FAIR, vulnerability describes knowledge about those landscapes, rather than a specific state of nature concerning system integrity. In FAIR, vulnerability is derived as an outcome of the difference between control strength and threat capability. So in FAIR, if a threat's capabilities are greater than the ability to resist, we have a significant degree of vulnerability. If, on the other hand, the ability to resist is greater than the threat's capability, we are significantly less vulnerable.

In contrast, ISO treats vulnerabilities as system or process weaknesses in a system.

3.6.3 Consideration for the vulnerability landscape
In considering vulnerability, creating a list of system or process weaknesses is useful information to be gathered for the development of a FAIR control

strength estimate. Analysts, however, are encouraged to think about vulnerability as a spectrum to describe the inherent uncertainty concerning the quality of threat landscape information.

3.6.4 Development of metrics for the vulnerability landscape

As mentioned earlier, vulnerability in FAIR is a derived value that describes knowledge about the threat landscape and the controls landscape. The means to arrive at a vulnerability estimate is included later in this guide.

Chapter 4 How to use FAIR in your ISMS

The Information Security Management System (ISMS) is fundamentally a process, composed of tasks that transform input information into desired outputs. Thus, a task cannot be performed before all of its required inputs are available. FAIR decomposes the calculation of risk into its components, which constrains the precedence for task sequence. A third influence on task sequence is the series of one-to-many relationships among the data elements found in FAIR. Figure 4.1 shows these relationships.

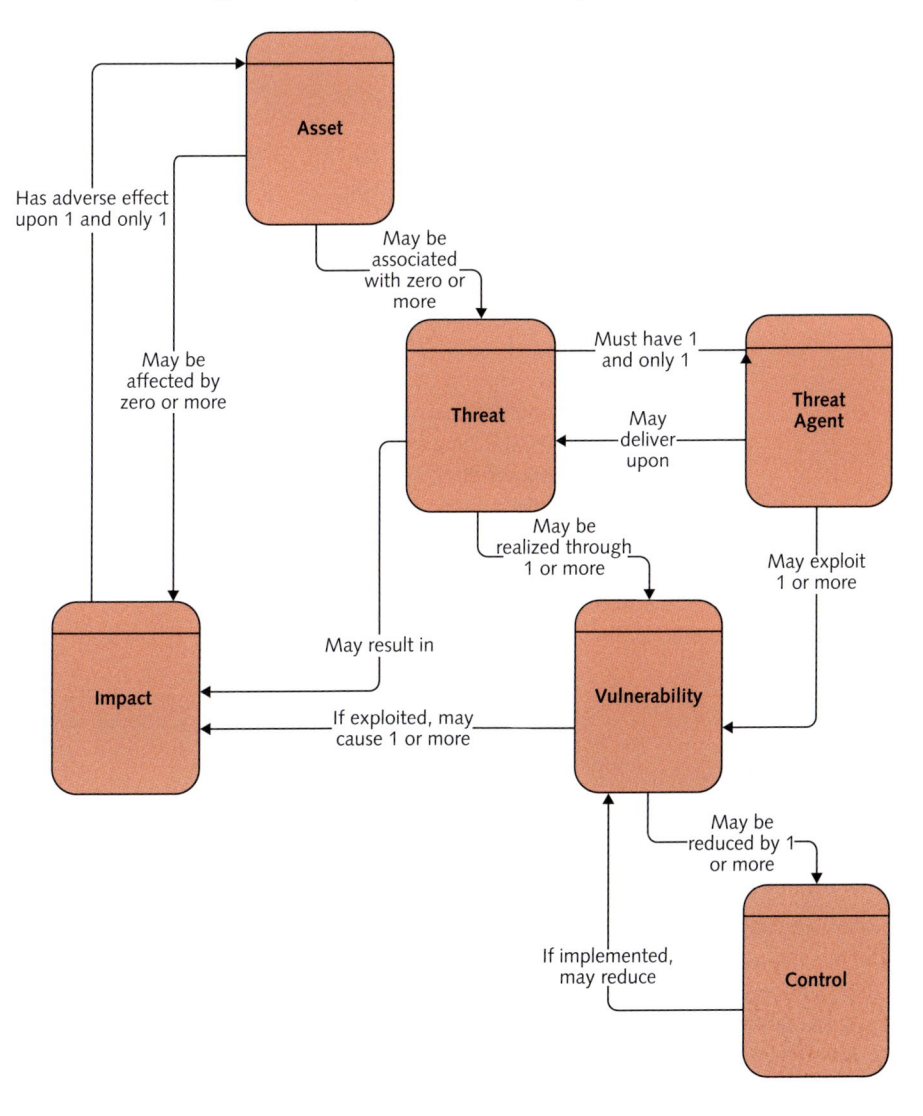

Figure 4.1: ISMS component relationships

4.1 Recipe for ISO/IEC 27005 risk management with FAIR

This section presents the process for risk management, focusing on the inputs, actions, and outputs (Table 4.1). You will see the sequence of steps that was provided in Chapter 2. Key input data (identified with underscores) was discussed in detail in Chapter 3. And this chapter provides the detailed explanation for the actions. Most of the text is drawn from ISO, with FAIR concepts *presented in italics*.

Table 4.1: ISO inputs, required actions, and outputs and how they can be used in FAIR

Inputs	Actions – ISO	Outputs
7.0 Context Establishment		
7.1 General Considerations		
All information about the organization relevant to establish the information security risk management context.	Establish the context for information security risk management: • Setting the basic criteria necessary for information security risk management (7.2) • Defining the scope and boundaries (7.3) • Establishing an appropriate organization operating the information security risk management (7.4)	A1 Specification of basic risk evaluation criteria A2 Scope and boundaries for risk analysis

Inputs	Actions – FAIR	Outputs
STAGE 1: Identify Scenario Components		
Identify the asset at risk:		
A2 Scope and boundaries for risk analysis + List of constituents with owners, location, function, etc.	1 *Identify each asset (e.g., information, application, etc.) and scope the asset (e.g., enterprise, business unit, etc.)*	B1 List of assets to be risk-managed
Identify the threat community:		
+ Information on threats, from reviewing incidents, asset owners, users, external threat catalogs, other sources	2 *For each asset, identify the threat agent (e.g., insiders such as employees, contract workers; outsiders such as spies, thieves, competitors)* 3 *For each threat agent, define the action and identify the contact* 4 *Record the title and description of the threat*	C1 List of threats, with identification of threat type and threat source C2 *Threat title and description*

Inputs	Actions – FAIR	Outputs
STAGE 2: Estimate Loss Event Frequency (LEF)		
Estimate probable Threat Event Frequency (TEF):		
B1 List of assets to be risk-managed C1 List of threats, with identification of evidences of frequency	5 Estimate the Threat Event Frequency (TEF) 6 For each threat, identify vulnerabilities that could be exploited by the threat agent	C3 Threat Event Frequency (TEF) E1 List of vulnerabilities in relation to assets, threats, and controls
Estimate Threat Capability (TCap):		
E1 List of vulnerabilities in relation to assets, threats, and controls	7 Estimate the threat's capabilities relative to each vulnerability	E3 Threat capability
Estimate Control Strength (CS):		
+ Documentation of controls + Documentation risk treatment implementation plans. E3 Threat capability	9 For each vulnerability, identify existing <u>controls</u> that reduce the vulnerability 10 Evaluate the control strength for each control	D1 Control Strength (CS) – List of all existing and planned controls, their effectiveness, implementation, and usage status
Derive Vulnerability (Vuln):		
D1 Control Strength (CS) – List of all existing and planned controls, their effectiveness, implementation, and usage status	11 Calculate Vulnerability (Vuln)	D2 Vulnerability (Vuln)
Derive Loss Event Frequency (LEF):		
C3 Threat Event Frequency (TEF) D1 List of all existing and planned controls, their effectiveness, implementation, and usage status D2 Vulnerability (Vuln)	12 Calculate Loss Event Frequency (LEF)	H2 Loss Event Frequency (LEF)
STAGE 3: Evaluate Probable Loss Magnitude (PLM)		
Estimate worst-case loss:		
Estimate Probable Loss Magnitude (PLM):		
C2 Threat title and description	8 Estimate potential <u>impacts</u> for each threat	G2 Probable Loss Magnitude (PLM) for each threat

Inputs	Actions – FAIR	Outputs
STAGE 4: Derive and Articulate Risk		
A1 Specification of basic risk evaluation criteria D2 Vulnerability (Vuln) H2 Loss Event Frequency (LEF) G2 Probable Loss Magnitude (PLM)	13 Calculate risk 14 Produce risk reports	I1 Risk J1 List of risks prioritized according to risk evaluation criteria in relation to the incident scenarios that lead to those risks J2 Prioritized control improvements

Inputs	Actions – ISO	Outputs
9.0 Information security risk treatment		
9.1 General description of risk treatment		
I1,J1 List of risks prioritized according to risk evaluation criteria in relation to the incident scenarios that lead to those risks	Select controls to reduce, retain, avoid, or transfer the risks Prepare a risk treatment plan	K1 Risk treatment plan K2 Residual risks subject to the acceptance decision of the organization's managers
9.2 Risk Reduction	Reduce risk by selecting controls so that the residual risk can be reassessed as being acceptable	
9.3 Risk Retention	Decide to retain the risk without further action, based on risk evaluation	
9.4 Risk Avoidance	Avoid the activity or condition that gives rise to the particular risk	
9.5 Risk Transfer	Transfer the risk to another party that can most effectively manage the particular risk, based on risk evaluation	

Inputs	Actions – ISO	Outputs
10.0 Information Security Risk Acceptance		
K1 Risk treatment plan K2 Residual risk assessment subject to the acceptance decision of the organization's managers	The decision to accept the risks and responsibilities for the decision should be made and formally recorded (this relates to ISO/IEC 27001 §4.2.1 (h)).	List of accepted risks with justification for those that do not meet the organization's normal risk acceptance criteria

Inputs	Actions – ISO	Outputs
11.0 Information Security Risk Communication		
All risk information obtained from the risk management activities	Information about risk should be exchanged and/or shared between the decision-maker and other stakeholders.	Continual understanding of the organization's information security risk management process and results

Inputs	Actions – ISO	Outputs
12.0 Information Security Risk Monitoring and Review		
12.1 Monitoring and Review of Risk Factors		
All risk information obtained from the risk management activities	Monitor and review risks and their factors (i.e., value of assets, impacts, threats, vulnerabilities, likelihood of occurrence) to identify any changes in the context of the organization at an early stage, and to maintain an overview of the complete risk picture	Continual alignment of the management of risks with the organization's business objectives, and with risk acceptance criteria
12.2 Risk Management Monitoring, Reviewing, and Improving		
All risk information obtained from the risk management activities		Continual relevance of the information security risk management process to the organization's business objectives or updating the process

4.2 Define the context for information security risk management

4.2.1 General considerations

Establish the context for information security risk management:

- Setting the basic criteria necessary for information security risk management (ISO/IEC 27005 §7.2)
- Defining the scope and boundaries (ISO/IEC 27005 §7.3)
- Establishing an appropriate organization operating the information security risk management (ISO/IEC 27005 §7.4)

The organization must have the resources to appropriately engage in a risk management process. These resources must include the following:
- Perform risk assessments
- Develop risk treatment plans
- Define and implement policies and procedures to implement selected controls
- Monitor implemented controls
- Monitor the overall risk management process

Without such resources, establishing a risk management process will set expectations of the organization that cannot be met.

This task should be performed from an organizational perspective for the overall development of the ISMS, but also considered for each risk assessment to ensure success of the risk assessment results.

4.2.2 Risk acceptance criteria

Developing a set of risk acceptance criteria based on the goals and objectives of the organization is important to have as an integral part of the ISMS. This assists in the development of risk treatment plans. Developing a list of risk acceptance criteria sets the groundwork for determining what risks the organization is capable of accepting, in general terms. This is probably done once when developing the ISMS, but may need to be adjusted for each risk assessment performed at the time of risk treatment plan development.

Risk acceptance criteria should be developed and specified. Risk acceptance criteria often depend on the organization's policies, goals, objectives, and the interests of stakeholders.

An organization should define its own scales for levels of risk acceptance. The following should be considered during development:
- Risk acceptance criteria may include multiple thresholds, with a desired target level of risk, but provision for senior managers to accept risks above this level under defined circumstances.
- Risk acceptance criteria may be expressed as the ratio of estimated profit (or other business benefit) to the estimated risk.
- Different risk acceptance criteria may apply to different classes of risk; e.g., risks that could result in non-compliance with regulations or laws may

not be accepted, while acceptance of high risks may be allowed if this is specified as a contractual requirement.
- Risk acceptance criteria may include requirements for future additional treatment; e.g., a risk may be accepted if there is approval and commitment to take action to reduce it to an acceptable level within a defined time period.
- Risk acceptance criteria may differ according to how long the risk is expected to exist; e.g., the risk may be associated with a temporary or short-term activity.

In developing the risk acceptance criteria, the following should be considered:
- Business criteria
- Legal and regulatory aspects
- Operational considerations
- Technological aspects
- Financial considerations
- Social and humanitarian factors

Place the organization's generalized risk acceptance criteria from the ISMS in Question 2 of the Risk Management Program Worksheet (Appendix A).

Consider whether there are specific risk acceptance criteria for the risk assessment under consideration in Question 3 of the Risk Management Program Worksheet (Appendix A).

4.3 Calculate risk

4.3.1 Stage 1
Identify each asset (e.g., information, application, etc.) and scope the asset (e.g., enterprise, business unit, etc.).

Describe the asset(s) and critical attributes under consideration
Identification and description of the assets under consideration during a risk assessment is critical. Identify the asset(s) under consideration during this risk assessment in Question 3 of the Risk Management Program Worksheet (Appendix A).

Describe the threats to the asset(s) under consideration

For each asset, identify the threat agent(s) (e.g., insiders such as employees, contract workers; outsiders such as spies, thieves, competitors) in the space provided in Question 4 of the Risk Management Program Worksheet (Appendix A).

For each threat agent describe the frequency with which threat agents may come into contact with the asset(s) under consideration in the space provided in Question 4 of the Risk Management Program Worksheet (Appendix A).

For each threat agent, estimate the probability that they will act against the asset(s) in the space provided in Question 4 of the Risk Management Program Worksheet (Appendix A).

Define the potential action and describe the threat(s) in the space provided in Question 4 of the Risk Management Program Worksheet (Appendix A).

4.3.2 Stage 2

Estimate the Loss Event Frequency (LEF)

The Loss Event Frequency (LEF) considers the following factors: Threat Event Frequency (TEF), Threat Capability (TCap), Control Strength (CS), and Vulnerability (Vuln).

Estimate the probable Threat Event Frequency (TEF)

Estimate the probable Threat Event Frequency (TEF). Use the information in Question 4 of the Risk Management Program Worksheet (Appendix A).

Table 4.2 shows the ratings for the values of the Threat Event Frequency (TEF). Circle the estimated Threat Event Frequency (TEF) in Question 5 of the Risk Management Program Worksheet (Appendix A).

Rating	Description
Very High (VH)	⤑ 100 times per year
High (H)	Between 10 and 100 times per year
Moderate (M)	Between 1 and 10 times per year
Low (L)	Between 0.1 and 1 times per year
Very Low (VL)	⬅ 0.1 times per year (less than once every 10 years)

Table 4.2: Ratings for the values of Threat Event Frequency

Estimate the Threat Capability (TCap)

Estimate the Threat Capability (TCap), which is the capability that the threat community has to act against the asset using a specific threat. Use the information in Question 4 of the Risk Management Program Worksheet (Appendix A).

Table 4.3 shows the ratings for the values of Threat Capability (TCap). Circle the Threat Capability (TCap) in Question 6 of the Risk Management Program Worksheet (Appendix A).

Rating	Description
Very High (VH)	Top 2% when compared against the overall threat population
High (H)	Top 16% when compared against the overall threat population
Moderate (M)	Average skill and resources (between bottom 16% and top 16%)
Low (L)	Bottom 16% when compared against the overall threat population
Very Low (VL)	Bottom 2% when compared against the overall threat population

Table 4.3: Ratings for the values of Threat Capability

Estimate the Control Strength (CS)

Estimate the Control Strength (CS), which represents the probability that the organization's controls will be able to withstand a baseline measure of force. Use the information in Question 4 of the Risk Management Program Worksheet (Appendix A).

Table 4.4 shows the ratings for the values of Control Strength (CS).

Rating	Description
Very High (VH)	Protects against all but the top 2% of an average threat population
High (H)	Protects against all but the top 16% of an average threat population
Moderate (M)	Protects against the average threat agent
Low (L)	Only protects against bottom 16% of an average threat population
Very Low (VL)	Only protects against bottom 2% of an average threat population

Table 4.4: Ratings for the values of Control Strength

Derive the Vulnerability (Vuln)

Derive the Vulnerability (Vuln) using the vulnerability matrix below (Figure 4.2). Locate the intersection of Threat Capability (TCap) and Control Strength (CS) from Question 6 and 7 of the Risk Management Program Worksheet (Appendix A). Circle the Vulnerability (Vuln) in Question 8 of the Risk Management Program Worksheet (Appendix A).

Vulnerability (Vuln)

Threat Capability (TCap)	VL	L	M	H	VH
VH	VH	VH	VH	H	M
H	VH	VH	H	M	L
M	VH	H	M	L	VL
L	H	M	L	VL	VL
VL	M	L	VL	VL	VL

Control Strength (CS)

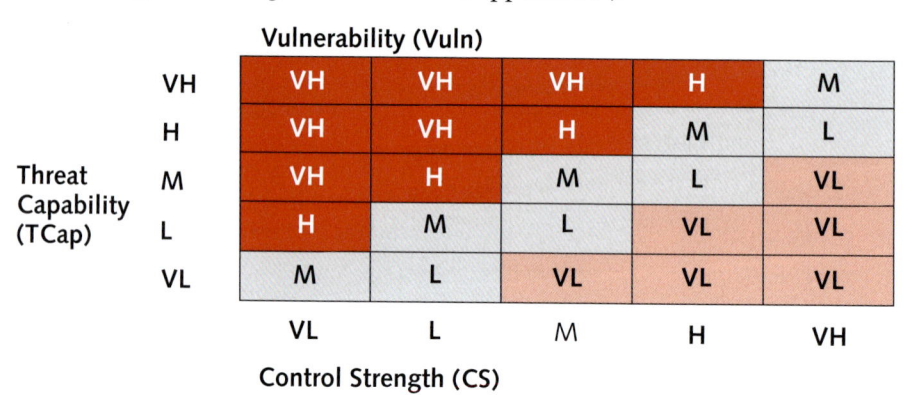

Figure 4.2: Vulnerability matrix

Derive Loss Event Frequency (LEF)

Derive the Loss Event Frequency (LEF) using the Loss Event Frequency (LEF) matrix below (Figure 4.3). Locate the intersection of Threat Event Frequency (TEF) and Vulnerability (Vuln) to derive Loss Event Frequency (LEF) from Question 5 and 8 of the Risk Management Program Worksheet (Appendix A). Circle the Loss Event Frequency (LEF) in Question 9 of the Risk Management Program Worksheet (Appendix A).

Loss Event Frequency (LEF)

		VL	L	M	H	VH
Threat Event Frequency (TEF)	VH	M	H	VH	VH	VH
	H	L	M	H	H	H
	M	VL	L	M	M	M
	L	VL	VL	L	L	L
	VL	VL	VL	VL	VL	VL

Vulnerability (Vuln)

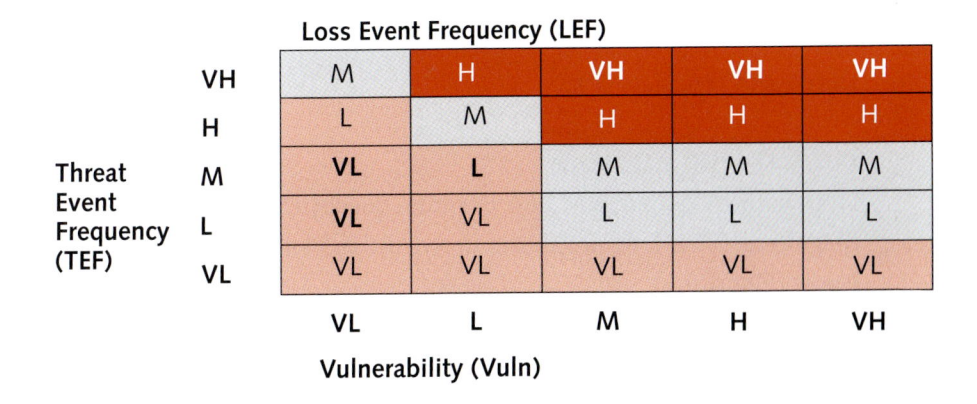

Figure 4.3: Loss Event Frequency matrix

4.3.3 Stage 3
Evaluate the Probable Loss Magnitude (PLM)

Determine the probable impact of the loss. This is identified as the Probable Loss Magnitude (PLM). This includes estimating the worst-case scenario as well as the most probable scenario(s) of loss.

Estimate the worst-case loss and Probable Loss Magnitude (PLM)

Use the values in Figure 4.4 below to determine the magnitudes for the worst-case scenarios and Probably Loss Magnitude (PLM) for each appropriate threat action and loss form. The range values should be adjusted appropriately to meet the needs of the organization.

Magnitude	Range Low End	Range High End
Severe (SV)	$10,000,000	–
High (H)	$1,000,000	$9,999,999
Significant (Sg)	$100,000	$999,999
Moderate (M)	$10,000	$99,999
Low (L)	$1,000	$9,999
Very Low (VL)	$0	$999

Figure 4.4: Values for worst-case loss and Probable Loss Magnitude (PLM)

For each threat action, enter the magnitude into the tables in Question 10 and 11 of the Risk Management Program Worksheet (Appendix A).

4.3.4 Stage 4

Derive and articulate risk.

Derive the risk magnitude

Once we have estimates of Loss Event Frequency (LEF) and Probable Loss Magnitude (PLM), we are able to derive the risk value from the risk matrix below (Figure 4.5).

This matrix is used to derive risk using Probable Loss Magnitude (PLM) and Loss Event Frequency (LEF). Identify the intersection of the Probable Loss Magnitude (PLM) and Loss Event Frequency (LEF) from Question 9 and 11 of the Risk Management Program Worksheet (Appendix A). Circle the Risk in Question 12 of the Risk Management Program Worksheet (Appendix A).

Risk

Probable		VL	L	M	H	VH
	Severe	H	H	C	C	C
	High	M	H	H	C	C
	Significant	M	M	H	H	C
	Moderate	L	M	M	H	H
	Low	L	L	M	M	M
	Very Low	L	L	M	M	M

Loss Event Frequency (LEF)

Key for Risk Values

Key	Risk Level
C	Critical
H	High
M	Moderate
L	Low

Figure 4.5: Risk matrix

Articulate the real risk

The real challenge has to do with articulating this risk value to the decision-makers. This can be performed using the information gathered through this entire process using the ISO/IEC 27005 communication framework.

A major consideration of communicating risk levels is the association of qualitative labeling with a tendency to equate "high-risk" with "unacceptable", and "low-risk" with "acceptable". In fact, in some circumstances high-risk is entirely acceptable (e.g., in cases where the potential for reward outweighs the risk). In other situations, a relatively low-risk condition may be unacceptable, particularly if the exposure is systemic within an organization. Including more specific information regarding Loss Event Frequency (LEF) and Probable Loss Magnitude (PLM) can help to reduce the bias associated with qualitative risk labels.

In summary, risk articulation must meet the needs of the decision-makers. When using qualitative labels for range values, it is imperative to ensure that management agrees with the criteria for each range/level.

4.4 Determine the appropriate information risk treatment plan

The four options available for risk treatment are:
- Risk Reduction – Actions taken to lessen the probability, negative consequences, or both, associated with a risk.
- Risk Avoidance – Decision not to become involved in, or action to withdraw from, a risk situation.
- Risk Transfer – Sharing with another party the burden of loss or benefit of gain, for a risk.
- Risk Retention – Acceptance of the burden of loss or benefit of gain from a particular risk.

The four options for risk treatment are not mutually exclusive. Sometimes the organization can benefit substantially by a combination of options.

Some risk treatments can effectively address more than one risk. A risk treatment plan should be defined which clearly identifies the priority ordering in which individual risk treatments should be implemented and their timeframes.

Using the determination of risk magnitude and the discussion of actual risk from Question 12 and 13 of the Risk Management Program Worksheet (Appendix A) and the Generalized Risk Acceptance Criteria in Question 2 of the Risk Management Program Worksheet (Appendix A), answer the question in Question 14 of the Risk Management Program Worksheet (Appendix A).

Using the information provided in Question 2 of the Risk Management Program Worksheet (Appendix A), assess whether the risk will be at an acceptable level for the organization once the treatment plan has been implemented. Circle the appropriate answer in Question 15 of the Risk Management Program Worksheet (Appendix A).

4.5 Develop an information security risk communication plan

The steps involved in risk communication is a bi-directional process designed to achieve agreement on how to manage risks by exchanging and/or sharing information about risk between the decision-makers and other stakeholders.

Effective communication among stakeholders is important since this may have a significant impact on decisions that must be made. Communication will ensure that those responsible for implementing risk management, and those with a vested interest, understand the basis on which decisions are made and why particular actions are required.

Perceptions of risk can vary due to differences in assumptions, concepts, and the needs, issues, and concerns of stakeholders as they relate to risk or the issues under discussion. Stakeholders are likely to make judgments on the acceptability of risk based on their perception of risk. This is especially important to ensure that the stakeholders' perceptions of risk, as well as their perceptions of benefits, can be identified and documented and the underlying reasons clearly understood and addressed.

Using all of the information gathered in the Risk Management Program Worksheet (Appendix A) as input, answer the items in Question 16 of the Risk Management Program Worksheet (Appendix A).

4.6 Describe the information security risk monitoring and review plan

Risks are not static. Threats, vulnerabilities, likelihood, or consequences may change abruptly without any indication. Therefore, constant monitoring is necessary to detect these changes.

Organizations should ensure that the following are continually monitored:
- New assets that have been included in the risk management scope
- Necessary modification of asset values; e.g., due to changed business requirements
- New threats that could be active both inside and outside the organization and that have not been assessed
- Possibility that new or increased vulnerabilities could allow threats to exploit these new or changed vulnerabilities
- Identified vulnerabilities to determine those becoming exposed to new or re-emerging threats
- Increased impact or consequences of assessed threats, vulnerabilities, and risks in aggregation resulting in an unacceptable level of risk
- Information security incidents

New threats, vulnerabilities, or changes in probability or consequences can increase risks previously assessed as low. Review of low and accepted risks should consider each risk separately, and all such risks as an aggregate as well, to assess their potential accumulated impact if risks do not fall into the low or acceptable risk category.

Answer the items in Question 17 of the Risk Management Program Worksheet (Appendix A).

Appendix A Risk Management Program Worksheet

A.1 Define the context for information security risk management
General considerations

1. Are the following resources available in the organization to support the risk management program?

Are resources available to conduct risk assessments?   Yes | No

Describe these resources below:
_____
_____

Are resources available to develop risk treatment plans?   Yes | No

Describe these resources below:
_____
_____

Are resources available to implement the selected controls?   Yes | No

Describe these resources below:
_____
_____

Are resources available to establish policies and procedures to support the selected controls?   Yes | No

Describe these resources below:
_____
_____

Are resources available to monitor the implemented controls?   Yes | No

Describe these resources below:
_____
_____

Are resources available to monitor the overall risk
management program?   Yes | No

Describe these resources below:
_____
_____

2. What are the organization's generalized risk acceptance criteria from the ISMS?
_____
_____

Are adjustments to the organizations risk acceptance
criteria necessary?   Yes | No

If yes, define the adjustments below:
_____
_____

A.2 Calculate risk

Stage 1: Identify scenario components of asset(s) and threat(s)
Identify each asset(s) (e.g., information, application, etc.) and scope the asset(s) (e.g., enterprise, business unit, etc.).

3. Describe the asset(s) under consideration:
_____
_____

Identify the threat community

4. Identify the threats that can affect the asset(s).

Describe the potential threat agents:
_____
_____

Describe the potential frequency with which threat agents may come into contact the asset(s):

_____
_____

Probability that threat agents will act against the asset(s):

_____
_____

Define the anticipated actions and describe the potential threat(s):

_____
_____

Stage 2: Evaluate Loss Event Frequency (LEF)

5. Estimate the probable Threat Event Frequency (TEF). Select the rating below:

   Very High (VH) High (H) Moderate (M) Low (L) Very Low (VL)

6. Estimate the probable Threat Capability (TCap). Select the rating below:

   Very High (VH) High (H) Moderate (M) Low (L) Very Low (VL)

7. Identify existing and planned controls:

   Describe controls:

   _____
   _____

   Estimate the Control Strength (CS) for the control state. Select the rating below:

   Very High (VH) High (H) Moderate (M) Low (L) Very Low (VL)

8. Derive the Vulnerability (Vuln) Level. Select the rating below:

   Very High (VH) High (H) Moderate (M) Low (L) Very Low (VL)

9. Derive Loss Event Frequency (LEF). Select the rating below:

   Very High (VH) High (H) Moderate (M) Low (L) Very Low (VL)

Stage 3: Evaluate Probable Loss Magnitude (PLM)

10. Estimate worst-case loss:

Threat Action	Loss Forms					
	Productivity	Response	Replacement	Fine Judgments	Competitive Advantage	Reputation
Access						
Misuse						
Disclosure						
Modification						
Deny Access						

11. Estimate Probable Loss Magnitude (PLM):

Threat Action	Loss Forms					
	Productivity	Response	Replacement	Fine Judgments	Competitive Advantage	Reputation
Access						
Misuse						
Disclosure						
Modification						
Deny Access						

Stage 4: Derive and articulate risk

12. Derive the risk level. Select the risk magnitude below:

    Critical (C) High (H) Moderate (M) Low (L)

13. Articulate and discuss the risk below:

A.3 Determine the appropriate information risk treatment plan

14. Define the Information Risk Treatment Plan.

Risk reduction methods

What actions will be taken to reduce the risks associated with the identified threats on the associated assets(s)?

What are the expected costs of these risk reduction activities?

What are the expected benefits of these risk reduction activities?

Risk avoidance methods

Based on the identified risks, will the organization avoid these risks by either withdrawing from this activity or discontinue participating in this activity? Yes | No

What are the expected costs or losses to the organization of avoiding this risk?

What are the expected benefits to the organization of avoiding this risk?

Risk transfer options

Describe the available options for transferring all or parts of the identified risks:

What are the expected costs of the identified risk transfer options?

What are the expected benefits of the identified risk transfer options?

Risk retention
Describe the risks that will be retained by the organization:

15. Is the risk at acceptable level?   Yes | No

A.4 Develop an Information Security Risk Communication Plan

16. Develop the Information Security Risk Communication Plan.

Who are the stakeholders that are required to approve the risk treatment plan?

Who are the decision-makers that are required to approve the risk treatment plan?

Describe the methods that will be used to communicate the risks to the identified stakeholders and decision-makers (i.e., risk reports, presentation, etc.):

Describe the documentation expected from the decision-makers to approve the risk treatment plan:

A.5 Describe the Information Security Risk Monitoring and Review Plan

17. Risk monitoring and review for the identified asset(s), threats(s), and vulnerabilities(s).

Describe the available resources and/or systems in place to monitor the risks, threats, and vulnerabilities identified through this process:

Describe how the change management process within the organization will be used to monitor assets included in this assessment:

Glossary

Term	Source	ISO/FAIR Definition
Action	FAIR	An act taken against an asset by a threat agent. Requires first that contact occurs between the asset and threat agent.
Activity	ISO/IEC 27005	Used synonymously with Process.
Asset	FAIR	Any data, device, or other component of the environment that supports information-related activities, which can be illicitly accessed, used, disclosed, altered, destroyed, and/or stolen, resulting in loss.
	ISO/IEC 27001 ISO/IEC 27002	Anything that has value to the organization.
Asset Factors	FAIR	See Factors, Asset.
Availability	ISO/IEC 27001	The property of being accessible and usable upon demand by an authorized entity.
Broad Spectrum Risk Analysis	FAIR	See Risk Analysis, Broad Spectrum.
Confidentiality	ISO/IEC 27001	The property that information is not made available or disclosed to unauthorized individuals, entities, or processes.
Contact	FAIR	Occurs when a threat agent establishes a physical or virtual (e.g., network) connection to an asset.
Contact Frequency	FAIR	The probable frequency, within a given timeframe, that a threat agent will come into contact with an asset.
Control	ISO/IEC 27002	Means of managing risk, including policies, procedures, guidelines, practices, or organizational structures, which can be of administrative, technical, management, or legal nature. NOTE: Control is also used as a synonym for safeguard or countermeasure.
Control Strength	FAIR	The strength of a control as compared to a baseline measure of force.
Environmental Factors	FAIR	See Factors, Environmental.
Factors, Asset	FAIR	Characteristics of the asset(s) that drive loss magnitude.
Factors, Environmental	FAIR	Characteristics of the environment in which the organization operates that drive loss magnitude.
Frequency, Loss Event	FAIR	The probable frequency, within a given timeframe, that a threat agent will inflict harm upon an asset.
Frequency, Threat Event	FAIR	The probable frequency, within a given timeframe, that a threat agent will act against an asset.
Guideline	ISO/IEC 27002	A description that clarifies what should be done and how, to achieve the objectives set out in policies.

Term	Source	ISO/FAIR Definition
Impact	ISO/IEC 27005	Adverse change to the level of business objectives achieved
Information Security	ISO/IEC 27001 ISO/IEC 27002	Preservation of confidentiality, integrity, and availability of information; in addition, other properties, such as authenticity, accountability, non-repudiation, and reliability can also be involved.
Information Security Event	ISO/IEC 27001 ISO/IEC 27002	An identified occurrence of a system, service, or network state indicating a possible breach of information security policy or failure of safeguards, or a previously unknown situation that may be security relevant.
Information Security Incident	ISO/IEC 27001 ISO/IEC 27002	An information security incident is indicated by a single or a series of unwanted or unexpected information security events that have a significant probability of compromising business operations and threatening information security.
Information Security Management System (ISMS)	ISO/IEC 27001	That part of the overall management system, based on a business risk approach, to establish, implement, operate, monitor, review, maintain and improve information security.
Information Security Risk	ISO/IEC 27005	See Risk, Information Security.
Integrity	ISO/IEC 27001	The property of safeguarding the accuracy and completeness of assets.
Likelihood	ISO/IEC 27005	Used synonymously with Probability.
Loss Event	FAIR	A loss event occurs when a threat agent's action (threat event) is successful in negatively affecting an asset.
Loss Event Frequency	FAIR	See Frequency, Loss Event.
Loss Factors, Primary	FAIR	Factors that drive loss magnitude based solely on the nature of the asset and the threat agent's action.
Loss Factors, Secondary	FAIR	Factors that drive loss magnitude based on organizational and environmental conditions.
Method	FAIR	A rule or orderly procedure used in carrying out a task or accomplishing an aim.
Methodology	FAIR	A system of methods and rules applied to work on a given subject.
Multilevel Risk Analysis	FAIR	See Risk Analysis, Multilevel.
Organizational Factors	FAIR	Characteristics of the organization that drive loss magnitude.
Policy	ISO/IEC 27002	Overall intention and direction as formally expressed by management.
Primary Loss Factors	FAIR	See Loss Factors, Primary.
Probability of Action	FAIR	The probability that a threat agent will act against an asset once contact has occurred.

Term	Source	ISO/FAIR Definition
Probable Loss Magnitude	FAIR	The probable magnitude of loss resulting from a loss event arising due to a threat agent's action.
Residual Risk	ISO/IEC 27001	See Risk, Residual.
Risk	FAIR	The probable frequency and probable magnitude of future loss.
	ISO/IEC 27002	Combination of the probability of an event and its consequence.
Risk, Derived	FAIR	Risk that is derived from the risk matrix using Probable Loss Magnitude (PLM) and Loss Event Frequency (LEF).
Risk, Information Security	ISO/IEC 27005	Potential that a given threat will exploit vulnerabilities of an asset or group of assets and thereby cause harm to the organization. NOTE: It is measured in terms of a combination of the likelihood of an event and its consequence.
Risk, Residual	ISO/IEC 27001	The risk remaining after risk treatment.
Risk Acceptance	ISO/IEC 27001	Decision to accept a risk.
Risk Analysis	ISO/IEC 27001 ISO/IEC 27002	Systematic use of information to identify sources and to estimate the risk.
Risk Analysis, Broad Spectrum	FAIR	Any analysis that accounts for the risk from multiple threat communities against a single asset.
Risk Analysis, Multilevel	FAIR	Any analysis that accounts for the risk from a single threat community against a layered set of assets (e.g., defense in-depth).
Risk Assessment	ISO/IEC 27001 ISO/IEC 27002	Overall process of risk analysis and risk evaluation.
Risk Avoidance	ISO/IEC 27005	Decision not to become involved in, or action to withdraw from, a risk situation.
Risk Communication	ISO/IEC 27005	Exchange or sharing of information about risk between the decision-maker and other stakeholders.
Risk Estimation	ISO/IEC 27005	Process to assign values to the probability and consequences of a risk.
Risk Evaluation	ISO/IEC 27001 ISO/IEC 27002	Process of comparing the estimated risk against given risk criteria to determine the significance of the risk.
Risk Identification	ISO/IEC 27005	Process to find, list, and characterize elements of risk.
Risk Management	ISO/IEC 27001 ISO/IEC 27002	Coordinated activities to direct and control an organization with regard to risk. NOTE: Risk management typically includes risk assessment, risk treatment, risk acceptance, and risk communication.
Risk Reduction	ISO/IEC 27005	Actions taken to lessen the probability, negative consequences, or both, associated with a risk.
Risk Retention	ISO/IEC 27005	Acceptance of the burden of loss or benefit of gain from a particular risk.
Risk Transfer	ISO/IEC 27005	Sharing with another party the burden of loss or benefit of gain, for a risk.

Term	Source	ISO/FAIR Definition
Risk Treatment	ISO/IEC 27001 ISO/IEC 27002	Process of selection and implementation of measures to modify risk.
Secondary Loss Factors	FAIR	See Loss Factors, Secondary.
Taxonomy	FAIR	A systematic description of the subcomponents and their relationships within a complex subject.
Threat	FAIR	Anything that is capable of acting in a manner resulting in harm to an asset and/or organization; for example, acts of God (weather, geological events, etc.), malicious actors, errors, failures.
	ISO/IEC 27002	A potential cause of an unwanted incident, which may result in harm to a system or organization.
Threat Agent	FAIR	Any agent (e.g., object, substance, human, etc.) that is capable of acting against an asset in a manner that can result in harm.
Threat Capability (Tcap)	FAIR	The probable level of force that a threat agent is capable of applying against an asset.
Threat Community	FAIR	A subset of the overall threat agent population that shares key characteristics.
Threat Event	FAIR	Occurs when a threat agent acts against an asset.
Threat Event Frequency	FAIR	The probable frequency, within a given timeframe, that a threat agent will act against an asset.
Threat Factors	FAIR	Characteristics of the threat agent that drive loss magnitude.
Vulnerability	FAIR	The probability that an asset will be unable to resist actions of a threat agent.
	ISO/IEC 27002	A weakness of an asset or group of assets that can be exploited by one or more threats.
Vulnerability, Derived	FAIR	Vulnerability (Vuln) derived from the vulnerability matrix using Threat Capability (TCap) and Control Strength (CS).

Index

-
$-value 65

A
abstraction
    level of 13, 14
accuracy. 52
action 16, 17
analysis. 60
    approach 10
    definitions 10
    terminology. 10
analysis, level of 78
analysis methodology 11
arithmetic functions. 54
articulate risk 100
assessment method
    differentiation of. 49
    risk-focused. 54
    variability of 49
assessment results
    sactionable. 55
    communication of 64
    comparison of. 48
    concise. 54
    feasible. 54
    meaningful 54
    prioritization. 55
asset 50
asset landscape 80
asset loss factors 23
asset volume 24
audience. XIV

B
belief statement. 51

C
calculate risk 95, 105
calculation 56
CAPEC. 9
case law 29
COBIT XIV
competitive landscape 28, 29
complexity. 78
Contact. 16
    Intentional. 16
    Random. 16
    Regular. 16
context 93
contract law. 29
controls landscape .84
control strength 84
Control Strength. 18, 19
COSO. XIV
cost/benefit comparison 64
CS 96, 97
CWE. 9

D
data. 79
data metrics. 44
defensible. 53
deny access 37
destruction 37
detection 27, 28
disclosure. 37
distribution 53

due diligence 26, 29
    best practices. 26
    industry standards 26

E

estimate
    distribution 11
    range. 11
external indemnity. .48
external loss factors .28
external stakeholders 28, 29

F

FAIR 31, 43, 62, 68
FAIR Integration Model 75
FAIR risk analysis. 74
fines and judgments. 29
flexibility 43
frequency. 58, 96

I

incident scenarios. 85
information risk treatment plan. 101, 108
information security risk. 3
information security risk
    communication plan 102, 109
information security risk
    monitoring and review plan 103, 110
internal protective measures. 48
interval scale 57
interview and questionnaire 60
ISMS. 70, 89
ISO/IEC 27001 . . . . VIII, 69, 70
ISO/IEC 27002 . . . . VIII, 69, 71
ISO/IEC 27005 . . . . VIII, 68, 71
iteration 79
ITIL XIV

L

landscape of risk 80
LEF 15, 96, 90, 106
legal and regulatory landscape 28, 29
likelihood factor 58
logical. 53
loss
    competitive advantage. 22
    fines/judgments .22
    forms of 22
    productivity. 22
    replacement. 22
    reputation 22
    response. 22
loss analysis 21
loss categories 86
Loss Event Frequency 15
Loss Event Occurrence 14
loss factor. 22
    asset 22
    external 22
    organization 22
    threat 22
loss frequency 3, 9
loss (impact) landscape 85
loss magnitude 3, 8, 9, 14, 25
loss probability 20

M

magnitude of loss 9
management of risk .77
measurement. 56
media 28, 29
metrics 88
misuse 37

N

nomenclature 69
nominal scale 57
non-probability sampling 62

O

OCTAVE XIV
operating assumptions. 50
ordinal scale 54, 57
organizational loss factors. 26

P

password strength. 19
PDCA. 71
PLM 15, 20, 99, 107
precision 52
primary loss factors 23
probabilities for risk. 52
probability. 17, 96
probability factor
    level of effort. 17
    risk 17
    value. 17
probability sampling 62
probable frequency of loss. 54, 63
Probable Loss Magnitude 15, 20
probable magnitude of loss 54, 63
problem space 13

Q

qualitative estimate. 11
qualitative scale. 56
quantitative estimate 11
quantitative scale 56

R

range. 53
ratio scale. 58

regulations. 29
repeatable results 53
Requirements for Risk Assessment
    Methodologies. VIII
response. 27
    containment 27
    recovery. 27
    remediation. 27
risk 15, 49
    definition of. 48
risk acceptance 7
risk acceptance criteria 94
risk analysis. 62
risk articulation 101, 107
risk assessment 11, 12
    business objective. 48
    calculation. 56
    measurement 56
    methods. 48
    nature and scope 60
    traits 51
risk assessment methodology. 77
risk avoidance 108
risk budgeting. 7
risk factor. 2, 13
risk factor variables 12
risk magnitude 100
risk management 90
    model. 12
Risk Management Framework 68
risk measurement. 7
risk nomenclature. 7
risk prioritization 7
risk reduction 108
risk reduction statistics 64
risk retention. 109
risk taxonomy. 51, 64
    overview 14

Risk Taxonomy VIII
risk transfer 108
risk treatment 63
root causes 63

S

sampling 62
secondary loss factors 23, 26
sensitivity
    competitive advantage 24
    embarrassment/reputation 24
    general 24
    legal/regulatory 24
severity 62
solution option 63
stakeholders 59
synthesis 60

T

taxonomical framework 3
taxonomy
    example 31
TCap 96, 97
TEF 15, 16, 96
testing 61
threat 49
    access 24
    deny access 25
    disclosure 25
    misuse 24
    modification 25
threat agent 96
threat capabilities 25

Threat Capability 18, 19, 25
Threat Capability to Violate 25
threat community 105
Threat Competence 25
threat competencies 25
Threat Event Frequency 15, 16
threat landscape 82
threat loss factor 24
    action 24
    competence 24
    internal or external to the
        organization 24
threat metrics 83
timeframe 58
timing 26

U

unintended disclosure 24

V

value/liability 23
    cost 24
    criticality 24
    sensitivity 24
Vuln 96, 98
vulnerability 49, 63
Vulnerability 15, 18, 20, 87

W

worksheet 104
worst-case loss magnitude 64
worst-case scenarios 99